Battleground Europe

NOR

CW00394549

OPERATION GOODWOOD

THE GREAT TANK CHARGE
JULY 1944

With the continued expansion of the Battleground series a **Battleground Series Club** has been formed to benefit the reader. The purpose of the Club is to keep members informed of new titles and to offer many other reader-benefits. Membership is free and by registering an interest you can help us predict print runs and thus assist us in maintaining the quality and prices at their present levels.

Please call the office 01226 734555, or send your name and address along with a request for more information to:

Battleground Series Club Pen & Sword Books Ltd,
47 Church Street, Barnsley, South Yorkshire S70 2AS

Battleground Europe
NORMANDY

OPERATION GOODWOOD

THE GREAT TANK CHARGE
JULY 1944

Ian Daglish

Pen & Sword
MILITARY

First published in Great Britain in 2004 by
Pen & Sword Military
an imprint of
Pen & Sword Books Ltd
47 Church Street
Barnsley
South Yorkshire
S70 2AS

Copyright © Ian Daglish, 2004

ISBN 1 84415 030 5

The right of Ian Daglish to be identified as Author of the Work
has been asserted by him in accordance with the Copyright, Designs and
Patents Act 1988.

A CIP catalogue record for this book is
available from the British Library

Typeset in Palatino

Printed and bound in the United Kingdom by CPI

For a complete list of Pen & Sword titles, please contact
Pen & Sword Books Limited
47 Church Street, Barnsley, South Yorkshire, S70 2AS, England
E-mail: enquiries@pen-and-sword.co.uk
Website: www.pen-and-sword.co.uk

CONTENTS

Dedication

After writing two classic histories of the Normandy Campaign, *The British Breakout* and *Hill 112*, Major J J How, MC, embarked on the story of Operation GOODWOOD. Sadly, his declining health prevented him from progressing beyond the first chapter before his death in December, 1986. The draft passed through various hands before reaching this author. This account of GOODWOOD is not the work Joe How would have written, especially as it focuses on the tank actions at the expense of his own 3rd Monmouths' part in the battle. But it is respectfully dedicated to his memory: an infantry officer whose writing continues to bring his experiences to life for later generations.

Introduction and Acknowledgements

The history of Guards Armoured Division records of 18 July, 1944,

> *The fighting throughout the day was extremely confused and it is not easy to give a coherent account of it.*[1]

This confession is unusual in its honesty. Many accounts of Operation GOODWOOD, and of the wider Normandy campaign, continue not only to confuse but also to misinform.

The view of the individual soldier in a modern battle is generally very limited, and personal memoirs written after the event frequently borrow from popular histories to flesh-out the story and add interest. Unit histories of the post-war years were sometimes written in haste while memories served, and understandably amplify the achievements of a specific regiment at the expense of others. So are sown the seeds of confusion about the 'bigger picture'. As to the detail, mis-identification by the British forces of enemy tanks, guns, and units was the rule rather than the exception. When some unit histories confuse 18 July with 19 July, one must treat their version of the precise timing or sequence of events with caution. A recent scholarly work on the Normandy campaign concludes that even the official British history was

> *...very unreliable. In fact many of the errors are of such nature that it must be doubted if the book was actually written as an honest attempt at disclosing the truth.*[2]

We know that the author of the Official History was denied access to various relevant papers. Even the Staff College GOODWOOD film studied by generations of British Army officers is not above criticism.

With the passing years, it has become possible for the historian to disentangle much of the story that was previously confused. Sadly, many modern accounts fail to do the necessary groundwork, instead relying on flawed secondary sources. A recently published history of the Normandy campaign confidently states:

> The British had developed the superb seventeen-pounder anti-tank gun which could fling an 87mm armour-piercing hollow-charge shell at great velocity, and this was enough to deal with any German panzer.

Three factual errors in one sentence: the bore was 76mm; the seventeen pounder never had a hollow-charge round; and the gun was by no means certain to penetrate the best German armour. Worse still, some recent American accounts of the campaign have been at best anecdotal and, at their worst, screenplays for television rather than history.

Does it matter? No historical account can be guaranteed free of errors. But this author believes that with the wealth of source material now available, inadequate research does the men who fought these battles a disservice. If this modest account of GOODWOOD can help old soldiers and younger readers alike to gain a better understanding of what happened on a Normandy battlefield during two hot July days, it will have succeeded in its aim.

This author is grateful to the custodians of the primary material so valuable to researchers: David Willey, Curator, and David Fletcher, Historian at The Tank Museum, Bovington; David Porter at the Tactical Doctrine Retrieval Cell; N.A.R.A. (The U.S. National Archives & Record Administration, Washington D.C.). Alderley Edge Library has consistently triumphed in locating out-of-print works needed by the author. Personal insights have come from several former soldiers on both sides of the action: Bill Close and Jim Caswell of 3rd Royal Tank Regiment; Richard Freiherr von Rosen and Alfred Rubbel of *503. schwere Panzer-Abteilung*. Mrs Hazel Thorpe generously contributed the diaries of her late husband Jack, which allow us glimpses of the thoughts of a 2nd Fife & Forfarshire Yeomanry tanker. Further help has come from the growing body of keen historians striving to solve the remaining puzzles of the Normandy campaign: Alain Verwicht, Didier Lodieu, Bernard Paiche, and Jean-Claude Perrigault. Charles Markuss has freely shared his deep knowledge of the German Army.

Particular thanks are extended to Philippe Wirton for access to his collection of 1940s battlefield photographs, and to Normandy historian and cartographer Kevin Baverstock for his help and encouragement. The author is grateful to Her Majesty's Stationery Office for permission to use Crown Copyright material. Photographs on page 135 are reproduced by kind permission of The Tank Museum. Cover art 'Prepare to Ram' is reproduced by kind permission of David Pentland.

Notes on terminology

Original documents are quoted as accurately as possible – in some cases with non-standard spelling or punctuation, or military abbreviations such as British Army 'tk' for tank, 'fmn' for formation and German '*Pz.Gr.*' for '*Panzer Grenadier*'. German unit titles and ranks are generally given in the German style. Also, German style is followed by referring to gun calibres in centimetres, vs. the Allied style of measuring calibre in inches or millimetres.

References

1. *The Story of the Guards Armoured Division*, Rosse & Hill, 1956, p 38.
2. *Normandy 1944*, Niklas Zetterling, 2000, ISBN 0-921991-56-8, p 9.

CHAPTER ONE

THE BATTLE

Operation GOODWOOD was an odd battle. Midway through a series of Field Marshal Bernard Law Montgomery's Normandy offensives, which more-or-less followed a similar pattern, GOODWOOD stands out. It was the biggest tank battle the British Army fought in the Second World War. Unlike most of Montgomery's 'set piece' battles, it was fought in a manner which presented major logistical difficulties. A departure from the close network of Normandy hedgerows, the battlefield itself was unusually open. And debate is destined to continue over GOODWOOD's outcome.

Was GOODWOOD an Allied failure? Many have said so. Some who participated on the side of the Allies felt that their sacrifices had not achieved much. The troops had other names for it, 'The Atlantic Roller', 'Tank Alley', and 'The Caen Carve-Up' were among them.[1]

One officer of the Fife and Forfar Yeomanry reacted to the GOODWOOD plan as 'the Charge of the Light Brigade all over again!' Another squadron commander, of the more experienced 3/Royal Tank Regiment, received 'quite a few caustic comments from the old hands' during his briefing, '...with reminders of the last time the battalion had taken part in a Balaclava-like charge at Mareth in the desert'.[2]

A more senior participant wrote afterwards of the 'death ride of the armoured divisions'[3] while others took their inspiration from Shakespeare, looking back on *'the summer of our discontent'*.[4]

From the Allied point of view, Operation GOODWOOD

yielded impressive casualties and even more impressive losses of equipment, while failing to provide the dramatic breakthrough that war-weary civilians at home awaited. Matters were made worse by early news reports of a clean rupture of the German defences. *The Times* headline on 19 July read,

> *Second Army breaks through – armoured forces reach open country – General Montgomery well satisfied.*

This created the misleading impression of Allied tanks pouring out onto the open country north of Falaise. 25 July brought an embarrassed retraction:

> *...the word 'break-through' used in early reports can only be said to have a limited meaning.*

Worse still, misunderstandings between Allies led to over optimistic hopes being raised; when these were dashed recriminations flew and American confidence in the British leadership was shaken.

The interest of GOODWOOD lies at several levels. The battlefield is largely unaltered and easily accessible with good road, sea, and air links; visitors in their thousands pass by every year on their way into Normandy or further afield in France. GOODWOOD was a major tank battle at a time when the strategy and tactics of armoured warfare were still very much under development, and a massed tank assault was inevitably a learning exercise. So too was the employment of strategic airpower as a tactical battlefield weapon. Some lessons would take time to be absorbed; some were not learned at all. But a number of the ideas tested during GOODWOOD did come to influence British tactics through the remainder of the war in North West Europe.

From the defenders' point of view, GOODWOOD was a stern test of German concepts of defence-in-depth, of the relative merits of superior weapons systems versus more numerous opposition, and of the ability of outnumbered defenders to hinder and stop a larger enemy force. The conduct of this defence was to remain an object of close study by NATO forces for a further half-century.

References

1. *The Fife and Forfar Yeomanry*, R J B Sellar, 1960, p 168-169.
2. *A View From the Turret*, Major Bill Close MC, 2002, ISBN 0-9533359-1-7, p 115.
3. *Caen Anvil of Victory*, Alexander McKee, 1964, p 285.
4. *The Battle For Normandy*, E Belfield & H Essame, 1965, p 141.

CHAPTER TWO

THE NORMANDY BATTLEGROUND

The Airborne Bridgehead

In the early hours of 6 June, 1944, the open ground to the north-east of Caen became the first battleground of the Normandy campaign. Minutes after midnight, John Howard's 2/Oxfordshire and Buckinghamshire Light Infantry (the 'Oxf and Bucks') landed in their gliders to seize the twin bridges over the Caen Canal and the Orne River. Shortly after came the main body of 6th Airborne Division, the parachute regiments descending over the wide open fields east of the two waterways. Raiding parties set out in jeeps from the landing zones to blow the Dives River bridges at Varaville, Robehomme, Bures, and Troarn, successfully cutting German reinforcement routes from the east. To the north a scratch body of paratroopers succeeded against all odds in capturing the coastal battery at Merville. However, none of these locations was held at the end of the day. Units pulled back to a tighter perimeter where battle lines hardened around a narrow bridgehead east of the Orne River. Even this small bridgehead was to be bitterly contested. In the weeks ahead, the 6th Airborne was reinforced by the famous 51st Highland Division. As the Highlanders began to lay minefields around their positions, the Germans shored-up their own defences and periodically counter-attacked.

Major John Howard's glider landed yards from the bridge over the Caen Canal.

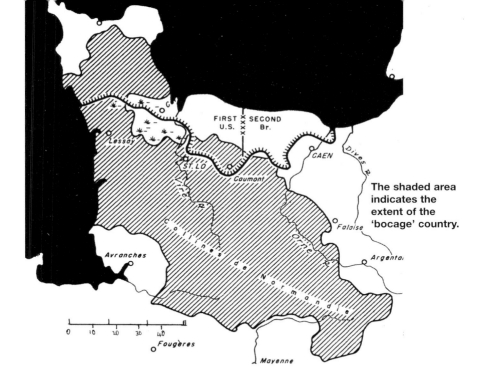

The shaded area indicates the extent of the 'bocage' country.

The Lie of the Land

It is important to understand the impact of the Normandy countryside on the development of the campaign. Directly inland from the British and Commonwealth landing beaches (Gold, Juno, and Sword) was an area of open plateau, as far south as Bayeux and beyond. Across this plateau on 6 June flowed the first British and Commonwealth forces clear of the beaches. By-passing some strongpoints in order to secure a deep beachhead, the leading units pressed on, liberating the town of Bayeux by the evening of the first day.

From Caen, a ridge runs south all the way to Falaise. Roughly mid-way between the Orne and Dives valleys, this ridge is open and gently undulating, broken only by occasional patches of woodland and frequent small villages. A major road runs arrow-straight down its back. The lack of obvious defensive terrain along this Falaise road strengthened the Germans' determination to conduct a forward defence close to Caen. Their first serious mobile counterstroke on the evening of 6 June was launched from the suburbs of Caen. Over the days and weeks, the German line held as newly arriving Axis reinforcements

13

coalesced around Caen into a solid defensive block.

Caen was the pivot. On that city hinged the whole German plan for the defence of Normandy. In front of the city, to the north-west, the open country was dotted with small villages of solid, stone buildings: Franqueville, Authie, Gruchy, Buron, St-Contest; each in its turn became a rubbled and bloody battleground before Canadian and British forces could pass. Due west of the city the fortified bunkers of Carpiquet airfield formed a citadel for the *Grenadiere* of *12. SS-Panzerdivision*, the open runways granting the defenders clear fields of fire. To the south-west, between the Odon and Orne river valleys, passage across the low but commanding Hill 112 was repeatedly denied to the British by powerful forces waiting on its reverse slopes to rebuff any assault. And all this time, north-east of Caen across the dual waterways of the Caen Canal and the Orne River, all attempts to expand the 6 June bridgehead were bitterly resisted.

For a British Army only recently mechanized, many of whose armoured units were officered by keen horsemen, the ideas of 'break out' and 'open country' were close partners. Beyond that small bridgehead east of Caen, across the Orne River and the Caen Canal, the open country along the Falaise road beckoned.

The flat battlefield viewed from the slopes of the Bois de Bavent, la Butte Verte.

CHAPTER THREE

ALLIED STRATEGY:
THE HINGE OF CAEN

Manpower and Morale

The failure to capture Caen on 6 June had major implications for the development of the campaign in north-west Europe. In the days following invasion, radical options were considered for taking the city. At an early stage, Montgomery proposed to drop 1st Airborne Division behind Caen to break the German line (a proposal rejected by Air Chief Marshall Sir Trafford Leigh-Mallory). Operation DREADNOUGHT considered a major assault around the east side of Caen, but was dismissed as offering too narrow an avenue of attack. Montgomery wrote to CIGS Alan Brooke on 19 June, expressing doubts which were to prove prophetic:

SECOND BRITISH ARMY

Detailed examination of the problem has revealed that the difficulties of forming up 8 CORPS in the bridgehead east of the R.ORNE, and of launching it from that bridgehead as the left wing of the pincer movement against CAEN, are very great.

The enemy is strongly posted on that flank and certain preliminary operations would be necessary, these would take time and we do not want to wait longer than we can help.

It has therefore been decided that the left wing of the pincer movement, from the bridgehead over the ORNE, shall be scaled down and be only of such a nature as can be done by the troops of 1 CORPS already there.

Accordingly, the veteran 51st Highland Division was inserted into the small perimeter to assist the depleted 6th Airborne: their joint objective to secure the Orne bridgehead rather than to break out. The 51st began to lay minefields in the open grain fields around their positions just as they had done in the open desert of North Africa.

General Bernard Montgomery

From the beginning of the campaign in north-west Europe, Montgomery knew that his Second British Army faced a potential manpower crisis. Once eight British infantry divisions were ashore[1], further infantry formations were not readily available. On 14 July, Montgomery wrote to inform the General Staff of his intentions for Operation GOODWOOD:

The Second Army is now very strong; it has in fact reached its peak and can get no stronger. It will in fact get weaker as the manpower situation begins to hit us.

For two years, British Army manpower intakes had failed to keep up with losses, and by mid-1944 Home Forces reserves were being bled dry. At the highest levels, manpower conservation was important. The General Staff response to Montgomery's letter was remarkably candid: 'General Montgomery has to be very careful of what he does on his eastern flank because on that flank (i.e., that of 21st Army Group) is the only British Army there is left in this part of the world.'

One recent study has summarized Montgomery's strategic challenge as being to '...obtain victory over Germany... with tolerable casualties and yet paradoxically with a high military profile'.[2] The longer the war went on, with British numbers continuing to dwindle, the greater would be the Americans' share of the resulting victory and their consequent influence over the post-war world. Meanwhile infantry losses exceeded projections. Montgomery's 14 June letter to the Imperial General Staff recognized:

...casualties have affected the fighting efficiency of the divisions; the original men were very well trained; reinforcements are not so well trained, and this fact is beginning to become apparent and will have repercussions in what we can do.

Particularly hard hit at the tactical level were the infantry officers. In the British Army of 1944, junior officers were required to run higher risks of injury than their men. Whether leaving cover to attend 'O Group' (orders) meetings, or simply moving from trench to trench around their men, exposed to enemy machine guns and mortars, officers and NCOs were vulnerable. After the early weeks in Normandy, officers learned to remove shoulder tabs and to carry maps folded into pockets instead of in distinctive map cases; back in Britain the 'Battle Schools' advised subalterns to carry a rifle or Sten gun. One tank commander was mistaken for a trooper by his brigadier, and 'I took this as a great compliment. If he couldn't tell a second

British numbers continued to dwindle with infantry losses exceeding projections.

lieutenant from a trooper, neither could a German sniper.' Nevertheless the junior officers were typically vulnerable in the forefront of any advance. Some infantry regiments got off to a good start. A successful first action could teach officers and men alike vital lessons that no amount of training had achieved; these combat veterans would be well placed to assimilate replacements into their ranks. But on a depressing number of occasions, an infantry unit's first assault would result in high casualties, with disproportionately high loss of officers who had worked alongside the men throughout the years of training and preparation.

One young infantry subaltern joined his platoon on 31 July: in place of the Establishment of thirty-six men he found only seventeen, of which twelve were recent replacements.

I sensed instantly that a tight grip was required, particularly so because those few who survived Hill 112 had witnessed what was, without doubt, the most horrific tragedy... Two of the NCOs... immediately reported to me and explained, forcefully

and in great detail, the poor state of the Platoon as they knew it to be. While they did so I was conscious of being weighed up. Was I fit to be their platoon commander? They were responsible, anxious and discriminating NCOs and my apprenticeship was to start immediately.[3]

Sidney Jary was lucky to inherit such capable NCOs, and repaid their trust by becoming a most capable leader. But not all platoons were so lucky. Once familiar NCOs and officers were gone, it was hard and sometimes impossible for unknown newcomers to bond the survivors and new replacements into cohesion and to help a shaken unit to regain its composure.

So it was in many units that the

early flush of enthusiasm for liberating Europe waned. In July, 1944, deteriorating morale became a major strategic consideration. After a month of bitter fighting in Normandy, many divisions were showing signs of battle fatigue. Indeed, some had not been in ideal shape on D-Day. In 50th Infantry some veterans had been resentful at being assigned to the initial assault and desertion rates grew high. 7th Armoured, the famous desert rats, experienced a disastrous engagement on 13 June, strung out along a country road outside Villers-Bocage when their lead elements were ambushed. The result was devastation. After this shock the division appeared to many to swing from reckless overconfidence to excessive caution. Even 51st Highland Division, Monty's 'highway decorators', fell briefly out of favour. Conditions were almost unbearable in the damp, mosquito-ridden trenches east of the Orne. Weeks of immobility under enemy fire and night bombing raids sapped the men's morale. It is worth noting that in the First World War British troops in the front lines were rotated in and out of action on a fairly regular basis, and often with comparatively pleasant rest areas close behind trench lines which remained static over long periods of time. The 51st Highland had no such relief. By mid-July, with no end to their torment in sight, men were disappearing before battle and officers resorted to threats of shooting runaways. Montgomery had to report the division 'at present not – NOT – battleworthy. It does not fight with determination and has failed in every job it has been given to do.' The commander was sacked and the 51st began the process of rebuilding morale.

Mobility

Prior to the invasion, Montgomery had talked confidently about the development of operations in Normandy following a successful lodgement on the coast.

Once the troops were ashore it was necessary for them to 'crack about'; the need for sustained energy and drive was paramount, as we had to link our beachheads and penetrate quickly inland before the enemy opposition crystallized. I gave orders that the leading formations should by-pass major enemy centres of resistance in order to 'peg out claims' inland.[4]

In reality, Montgomery himself soon realised that the terrain was not conducive to 'cracking about'.

General Sir Miles Dempsey.

It is often hard to separate Montgomery's confident pronouncements from his true assessment of the situation. Certainly, the 13 June debacle of Villers-Bocage made it abundantly clear to him that Normandy was not a battleground where freewheeling manoeuvre was likely to reap rewards. There had been some ineptitude in 22nd Armoured Brigade's attempt to exploit a gap in the German line. And, but for the alacrity of *Panzer Lehr Division* in filling the gap, a major British success might have resulted. Still, Montgomery attributed the failure to excessive boldness and lack of concern for flank cover. Thereafter security became his watchword. Future operations would be conducted with careful attention to securing flanks, advances being kept within reach of artillery bombardment. Montgomery's loyal Second Army commander General Miles Dempsey was not quite so cautious in his strategic assessment, occasionally entertaining more ambitious objectives than his master. At GOODWOOD, this difference of attitude would have unfortunate consequences.

The Holding Strategy

The Germans defending Normandy were resolute in denying Caen to the Allies. Having identified a prize that the defenders did not dare relinquish, Montgomery continued to threaten it in order to tie down the majority of the German armoured divisions.

Up to the end of June there was a sound operational need for the British to keep the German armour engaged. The German aim in this period was to assemble strategic reserves for a determined push through the Allied lines to the Channel. In the last week of June, the formidable *I. SS-Panzer Korps* was to be joined by *II. SS-Panzer Korps*, the strongest single formation in the theatre, fresh from its blooding in Cilicia. This 'gathering of the clans' was only pre-empted by Montgomery's Operations MARTLET and EPSOM. The Germans were forced to commit the newly arrived *9.* and *10. SS-Panzerdivisonen* piecemeal. As their component battalions arrived on the battlefield, without enjoying time to organize properly, these élite forces were flung into the attack across killing fields ploughed by British army and naval artillery. After EPSOM, *II. SS-Panzer Korps* remained a formidable adversary. But instead of forming a strategic reserve, its divisions were now required to hold their parts of the defensive line.

After EPSOM, the challenge changed from the operational to the strategic. No longer was it sufficient to draw the *Panzer* divisions out of reserve into holding the line. Montgomery now dictated that they should be held in the 2nd Army sector, directly in front of the British and Canadian forces. Montgomery took the view that the German defence of Normandy took the form of a doorway, with Caen its hinge. His options were either try to unhinge the door at Caen; to smash through the fabric of the door close to its hinge; or else to apply the laws of physics to lever the door open by applying force to the door handle. By July, Montgomery was wedded to the third option. He would maintain pressure on the hinge, holding the strongest German units in the east, but the decisive blow would ultimately be struck in the west. Then, to continue the analogy,

> ...mobile forces could pour through the gap and sweep round to take in the rear those Germans who still had their shoulders to the door close to the hinge, and dare not let go for fear of being

Failed plans up to the end of June 1944.

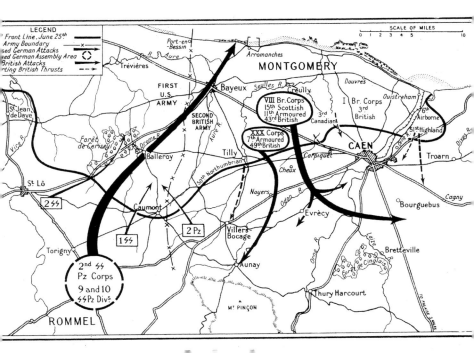

crushed if it were to swing violently back.[5]
Unfortunately, this was not the American view; and it was American forces on the Allies' right flank which would be swinging the door around.

Phase Lines and Personality Clashes

The original COSSAC plan envisaged simultaneous advances from the beach-heads: the Americans south to Avranches, while the British took the road from Caen to Falaise. This was reflected in 'phase lines', predicting steady development of the front in all directions. Eisenhower remained wedded to the idea of breakout by constant and steady application of pressure the whole length of the front. Eisenhower was not a tactician. His background in strategic planning con-trasted with Montgomery's combat experience. Eisenhower felt it his job to encourage continuous pressure, exerted the

General Eisenhower.

whole length of the front, supported by superior logistics, which would eventually stretch the defenders to the point at which their line would snap. As his chief of staff later commented:

> *He was up and down the line like a football coach, exhorting everyone to aggressive action.*[6]

Eisenhower and his staff found it hard to come to terms with the British preference for the occasional 'big push' preceded by logistic build up and followed by a pause to regroup before another set-piece push somewhere else. In Eisenhower's mind, 'constant aggressive action everywhere' was required; relations were not helped when Montgomery publicly dismissed this as a 'futile strategy'. While American forces struggled to advance through the marshy bocage of the Cotentin, Eisenhower looked to 21st Army Group to make similar efforts to achieve territorial gains along its front.

This, Montgomery would not do. In 1914, Montgomery had accompanied the British Expeditionary Force to war as a lieutenant in the Royal Warwickshire Regiment. In the trenches of the First World War he had witnessed the outcome of the French General Foch's policy that 'to make war always means attacking'. This philosophy was continued into 1917 by General Nivelle, who claimed to have found the 'secret of victory' in the 'attaque brusqée'. Hasty Nivelle's attack may have been; secret it was not.

> *In accordance with French practice exact details of the whole business had been broadcast through the customary network of wives and mistresses of those planning it.[7]*

Montgomery later wrote with feeling, 'Of all this I was a witness: I suffered from it. I saw clearly that such tactics could not be the key to victory.'[8]

He would not waste the manpower and morale of 21st Army Group in a war of attrition focused on small territorial gains. He preferred destroying the enemy to taking ground. Yes, there would be a price to pay:

> *The country in which we are fighting is ideal defensive country; we do the attacking and the Boche is pretty thick on the ground. I would say we lose three men to his one in our infantry divisions.*

But Montgomery would strive to conduct his campaign efficiently: both for reasons of personal conviction; and for the wholly practical purpose of preserving the morale and manpower of the British and Commonwealth forces for the eventual advance to the Seine and beyond.

In fairness, it should be recognized that neither Montgomery nor Bradley ever agreed to conform to 'phase lines'. Both men later claimed that these were necessary for logistical planning and not operational objectives. Also, a more rational German strategy for the defence of Normandy might have involved German forces giving up ground as the OVERLORD planners predicted: to shorten lines of supply, consolidate the front behind natural barriers, and move out of range of the devastating Allied naval artillery. But in the event rational strategy (*militärische Logik)* was to count for less than the inflexible will of the Führer.

While Eisenhower and the American generals remained disappointed by lack of visible progress in the east, Eisenhower's deputy, Air Chief Marshal Sir Arthur Tedder had his own criticisms of Montgomery. In Northern Africa, the Desert Air Force led by Tedder, and later by his successor Air Vice Marshal Arthur Coningham, had made great strides in developing co-operation with the army. Later, Tedder and

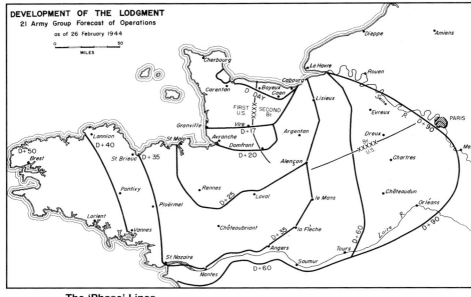

The 'Phase' Lines.

**Air Chief Marshal
Sir Arthur Tedder**

**Air Marshal
Leigh-Mallory.**

Coningham (and others besides) criticized Montgomery's cautious advance after his victory at Second Alamein. And criticism turned to resentment as Montgomery became a national hero whose 8th Army gained all the credit for winning the desert war. As the junior of the three services, the Royal Air Force was still sensitive to slights. Particularly irksome in the run-up to Overlord was Montgomery's sending his deputies to meetings with the air chiefs while he conducted his tour of the Army units. Tedder questioned whether the field marshal was really building morale or was in fact indulging in egotistical self-publicity.

Early in the Normandy campaign, Tedder and Leigh-Mallory seized on the issue of unachieved phase lines, pressing Montgomery to advance so that new airfields could be constructed south of Caen. Montgomery refused. Through his 21st Army Group Chief of Staff Major General F W de Guingand, Montgomery told the air chiefs that the *Luftwaffe* was not the threat that had been feared; 21st Army did not

24

require the airfields; and he would not allow his strategy to be dictated by unnecessary distractions. Montgomery was right. The *Luftwaffe* had not proved itself a sufficient threat to require the urgent building of airfields. But his lack of tact was insufferable. Resentment festered.

Charnwood

In the first week of July, Eisenhower wrote to Montgomery. 'We must use all possible energy in a determined effort to prevent a stalemate.' He feared the prospect of the Normandy campaign bogging down, or worse, 'fighting a defensive battle with the slight depth we now have'.[9] Monty responded with his accustomed confidence. He reassured the Supreme Commander that there was no question of a stalemate, and went on to detail his plans for another assault on German-held Caen.

The Field Regiments of the Royal Artillery were equipped with the 25-pounder gun-howitzer. This versatile weapon was to serve with distinction throughout the war. It could strike with pinpoint accuracy; it could sustain a prolonged barrage; it even had some antitank capability, which had proved invaluable in the desert fighting. Against enemies in the open, the 25-pounder could be devastating. But the 25-pound High Explosive shell was insufficient to crack open fortified positions. At best, a sustained bombardment could sap the defenders' morale, and keep heads down while infantry and armour closed in.[10] Winkling the *Panzergrenadiere* of 12.SS *Hitlerjugend* division out of their bunkers north and west of Caen required more. Montgomery turned to the Royal Air Force to facilitate Operation CHARNWOOD.

Eisenhower enthusiastically backed the request to divert strategic bomber forces, and the air planners devised a bomb line sufficiently far away (6,000 yards ahead of the Canadian assault) to minimize friendly losses. Between 21.50 and 22.30 hours on 7 July, 460 aircraft of RAF Bomber Command dropped 2,300 tons of High Explosive on a rectangle 4,000 by 1,500 yards. Six hours after this, just before dawn on 8 July, three Canadian and British divisions began a head-on assault. By 9 July, Allied troops at last penetrated the ruins of Caen as far as the left bank of the Orne River, where all further movement ground to a halt in the rubble. Tactically, the aerial bombardment was a failure. It fell behind the German defences. (In contravention of pre-

Caen received a pounding at the hands of the RAF.

invasion agreements on the preservation of important French sites, it devastated the city of Caen.) It actually discouraged a German withdrawal, while hindering the eventual Allied advance as roads were clogged by rubble. And far too much time elapsed between the bombing and the beginning of ground operations. But it nevertheless set a precedent.

References

1. Note: these were 3rd, 15th (S), 43rd, 49th, 50th, 51st (S), 53rd, & 59th, plus 6th Airborne Division, which was to play an active role in the campaign to the end of August.
2. *Montgomery and 'Colossal Cracks'*, Stephen Ashley Hart, 2001, ISBN 0-275-96162-1, p 6.
3. *18 Platoon*, Sydney Jary, 1987, ISBN 0 9512078 0 6.
4. *Normandy to the Baltic*, Field Marshall The Viscount Montgomery, 1946, p 31.
5. *The Struggle for Europe*, Chester Wilmot, 1952, p 370.
6. Bedell Smith, June, 1946.
7. *A New Excalibur*, A J Smithers, 1986, ISBN 0-436-47520-0, p 96.
8. *A History of Warfare*, Montgomery of Alamein, 1968, p 461.
9. *Breakout and Pursuit*, Martin Blumenson, 1961, Library of Congress 61-6000, p 119.
10. *Raising Churchill's Army*, David French, 2000, ISBN 0-19-924630-0, p 90-91.

Bombing Caen made the streets difficult to negotiate.

CHAPTER FOUR

THE GOODWOOD PLAN

Planning for Breakout

United States Army planning and equipment was based on mobility. General Bradley was confident that 'With the mobility and firepower we had amassed... we could easily outrun the German in an open war of movement.'[1]

But after a month in Normandy, the only American advances were still being made by slowly bludgeoning forward, at great cost. The prize of St-Lô was finally won on 18 July, not by any sophisticated manoeuvre but by two full divisions grinding relentlessly forwards 500 yards per day for eight whole days (also by the German defenders pulling out of the place before von Kluge, taking over from Rommel, could countermand the withdrawal). General Bradley bemoaned:

> No one disliked more than I did the disagreeable necessity for inching our way through those St-Lô hedgerows and Carentan marshlands. For while we sloughed afoot towards the Périers road, our vastly superior motorized equipment lay wasted under its camouflaged nets.[2]

What was needed was breakout. A decisive rupture of the German defensive lines that would allow the pent-up mobile forces to flow through in an unstoppable torrent. The alternative was to risk successful German containment of the Normandy bridgehead with all that entailed: reversion to static trench warfare while V Bombs threatened the awful possibility of a negotiated settlement with Nazi Germany. Bradley and his generals worked through the night on a plan.

On 10 July, Montgomery held a conference in his headquarters caravan at which General Bradley presented both bad news and good. The bad news was the slowness of the American advance, bogged down in the bocage country. Ahead of Bradley's Army lay miles of dense terrain, and German infantry reinforcements beginning to arrive from southern France. Behind lay supply bottlenecks as efforts continued to reopen the port of Cherbourg. And from above, the persistent bad weather had wrecked the American 'MULBERRY' (the artificial harbour transported from England) and limited air support from the English airfields. Bradley could not promise another major offensive until supplies were built up. But he brought one ray of hope for the future. With his closest advisors he had devised the outline of a plan for eventual breakout, the plan which was to become COBRA. The first step was to take the strategic town of St-Lô. Then, the dead-straight road that ran westwards from St-Lô to Périers would form a start line. Along that start line would be delivered the Americans' chosen solution to achieve breakthrough: carpet bombing. Operation COBRA would begin with a massive aerial bombardment by strategic as well as tactical air forces. The British were supportive of the idea. Montgomery (still in command of all ground forces) sympathized with Bradley's predicament and benevolently told him to 'take all the time he needed.'[3] Montgomery was formally to approve the plan on 18 July, whereafter the following day Bradley flew to England to brief the air chiefs at Stanmore. Air Chief Marshall Leigh-Mallory, usually resistant to any interruption of the strategic bombing of Germany, gave his full support, and Bradley left with:

...air's commitment for a far heavier blitz than I had dared dream of... altogether a total of 2,246 aircraft for five square miles of Normandy hedgerow.[4]

As the plan came together, American hopes turned to real optimism that, once cracked open, the German front might shatter, permitting exploitation as far as the ports of Brittany.

At the 10 July meeting, Dempsey listened with interest to Bradley's explanation of the delay in achieving a breakout. For all Montgomery's assurance to Bradley to take 'all the time he needed', Dempsey knew the importance of a speedy solution in Normandy. He proposed to Montgomery that second Army should also attempt their own

breakout. Montgomery refused to agree with an idea that ran so counter to his master plan. But Dempsey remained enthusiastic, and once again looked at the narrow corridor east of the Orne River. An attack there would present major logistical difficulties, but it was beyond all argument the furthest Allied-held ground from the planned COBRA offensive. Montgomery was not convinced. But, looking at the idea in the light of support for COBRA, his interest was rekindled. Ultimately, he directed Dempsey to form a corps of three armoured divisions and hold them disengaged, ready for a new offensive... east of the Orne River. By 13 July this was done: VIII Corps was holding 7th, 11th, and Guards Armoured divisions in reserve.

Montgomery had achieved the very benefit that his strategy denied the Germans: the ability to take a corps-level armoured force out of the line, disengaging it from day-to-day action in order to commit it to a strategic offensive. The point of the offensive was clear to Montgomery. His strategic objective for Operation GOODWOOD was to draw major German armoured formations on to the British front and hold them in the Caen sector while the American Operation COBRA achieved

Americans advance on St-Lô.

breakthrough in the west. But the clarity of this objective was to become muddied by subsequent events.

The Objectives of GOODWOOD

Montgomery's order to Dempsey read:

> *2 Army will retain the ability to operate with a strong armoured force east of the River Orne in the general area between Caen and Falaise... The immediate objective will be the plateau south east of Caen.*

For Montgomery, Falaise was a very distant goal; but on 13 July, Dempsey's Chief of Staff passed to O'Connor's VIII Corps an order which placed a significant interpretation on the wording. The order read:

> *'8 Corps will attack southwards and establish an armoured division in Bretteville-sur-Laize, Vimont, Falaise.'*

Suddenly, from being the general direction, Falaise was mentioned as an immediate objective.

Dempsey appears to have retained a genuine belief in his previous plan that a breakthrough on the British front was a strong possibility. In this he was encouraged by faulty intelligence which understated the strength (and depth) of the German defences facing Caen. He urged O'Connor to push the armour ahead. Whereas high infantry losses could not be afforded, he could afford to be profligate with the tanks, which were plentiful. He famously declared himself 'prepared to lose two or three hundred tanks.' What was more, the avenue of attack might be awkward to reach, but once begun GOODWOOD was to be fought over 'good tank country'. The open country of the Caen-Falaise plateau appeared to offer a way forward free of the constraints of the bocage that had so hampered previous offensives.

Montgomery was quick to correct his general. After viewing Dempsey's 13 July Operational Order, he issued a personal memorandum entitled *Notes on Second Army Operations 16th – 18th July* (the originally planned dates), hand-written in what VIII Corps' historian called 'his usual terse and succinct style'.[5] The note was intended as a clarification of Montgomery's original intentions. These were:

> *To engage the German armour in battle and 'write it down' to such an extent that it is of no further value to the German as a basis of the battle.*

> *To gain a good bridgehead over the Orne through Caen and thus to improve our positions on the eastern flank.*
>
> *Generally to destroy German equipment and personnel, as a preliminary to a possible wide exploitation of success.*

In later years, Montgomery was to fall back this document as 'proof' of his limited intentions for GOODWOOD. Ironically, however, its last few words kept the flame of Dempsey's imagined breakthrough alive, as Montgomery went on to suggest:

> *The three armoured divisions will be required to dominate the area Bourguebus-Vimont-Bretteville [sur Laize], and to fight and destroy the enemy, but armoured cars should push far to the south towards Falaise, spread alarm and despondency and discover 'the form'.*

Still, the prize of Falaise hung before Dempsey. A British penetration so far behind the German lines would surely destabilize the whole German defence of Normandy and trigger the run to the Seine so longed for. Dempsey passed the note on to O'Connor on 15 July, and as briefings rippled down through the organization, Falaise was repeatedly mentioned as the goal.

Doubts and Misunderstandings

Not only at lower level was there the makings of a serious misunderstanding, for while Dempsey's Operational Order was passed up the line to SHAEF (Supreme Headquarters Allied Expeditionary Force), Montgomery's hand-written clarification down to Dempsey and O'Connor's VIII Corps was not. Eisenhower became convinced that GOODWOOD was to deliver major a breakthrough, effectively a left hook through the German lines to mirror the right cross of Operation COBRA. It is unlikely that Montgomery intentionally set out to deceive Eisenhower. But he took no steps to correct the misunderstanding, which suited his purposes very well.

Like COBRA, Operation GOODWOOD was to be opened with a large-scale air attack on the German positions, although the reasons were somewhat different. Since an offensive east of the Orne required transferring all the attacking units to the east of the Orne, artillery back on the left bank of the river would be severely hampered. Montgomery supported Dempsey's request for heavy air support using extravagant language. To Eisenhower he promised that his *'whole eastern flank'* would *'burst into flames'*[6]; to Tedder that:

> *...if successful the plan promises to be decisive and therefore it is necessary that the air forces should bring their full weight to bear.*[7]

Expectations raised, Eisenhower's response was unrestrained:

> *I am viewing the prospects with the most tremendous optimism and enthusiasm. I would not be at all surprised to see you gaining a victory that will make some of the 'old classics' look like a skirmish between patrols.*

Even Tedder promised full support for the *'far-reaching and decisive plan'*. However, Eisenhower's response contained a clue to his misunderstanding. He promised Montgomery that the Americans would keep

> *...fighting like the very devil, twenty-four hours a day, to provide the opportunity your armored corps will need.*

This of course was the very reverse of the GOODWOOD objective: taking pressure off the Americans in preparation for *their* breakthrough.

Good Tank Country

Dempsey's plan for GOODWOOD was influenced by three main concerns. The first was the need to occupy and hold the *Panzers* on the British front (while being ready to seize any opportunity for a British breakthrough which might present itself). The second and third considerations represented experiments in the use of armour in battle. Both now appear, with the benefit of hindsight, to have been mistaken. Dempsey was persuaded both that armour alone might do the job (sparing the casualties to be expected if infantry took the lead); and linked to this he and others believed that the flat, open fields southeast of Caen were *'good tank country'*.

At the time GOODWOOD plan was developed, different theories were evolving about the use of armour on the battlefield, an art still less than three decades old. One legacy of

'Good Tank Country.'

the First World War was an acceptance that tanks in support of infantry could improve the chances of success while reducing infantry casualties. This was certainly true. Yet another deeply engrained belief was that the tanks' own success was conditional on the sort of ground on which the battle was fought. Flat, open ground was considered *'good tank country'*. This idea was understandable. In 1916, the first tanks ever sent into battle had to negotiate a wire-strewn quagmire pitted with craters and riven with trenches. Not for nothing was the Tank Corps flag a tricolour of brown, red, and green. First unfurled on the morning of 20 November, 1917, General Elles' standard heralded the first massed breakthrough of tanks from the morass of trench warfare, and gave the Corps its proud motto: 'through mud and blood to the green fields beyond'.

Cambrai became legendary. The spirit of centuries of

mounted cavalry was invoked: ...give us 'good country' and we can fight a mobile war.

In the few days available to the GOODWOOD planners, aerial photographs of the ground were carefully studied. The conclusion was that the open, rolling wheatfields would permit a rapid advance. Fields were intersected by hedges that tanks could easily cross. The only barriers visible were railway lines running at right angles to the line of the advance; these too it was felt should present little difficulty to the tanks. The planners were optimistic. But in fact, the GOODWOOD battlefield was far from being the 'good tank country' they sought, and might nowadays be considered among the worst terrain imaginable for a tank-heavy assault.

The approach to the battle was awkward. Even with extra bridges built across the Orne River and Caen Canal, the crossings were a bottleneck slowing the deployment of the attacking force. And deployment could not be begun before the start of the battle without abandoning all hope of surprise (a forlorn hope, as it happened) or incurring huge risk by massing formations in dense 'car parks' within range of enemy artillery and air attack. Limited access to the battle meant that the three armoured divisions would have to attack in sequence, one behind the other. And even in single file, each division would have to begin its advance through a limited number of narrow paths cleared through minefields. Worse, even when clear of the minefields, the battlefront itself was so narrow that there was not even room to deploy a full division. The initial advance down the narrow corridor would barely permit the deployment of two squadrons (about forty tanks) in line abreast.

It was predicted that bombardment, and especially aerial bombing, would be sufficient to suppress the defenders of the small Norman villages to either side of the corridor, at least long enough for the follow-up infantry to secure the flanks of the armoured break-in. It was assumed that the railway crossings would present no major problems. It was hoped that after the tanks had penetrated the crust of the German defences, they would be 'in the clear'. In every one of these particulars, the GOODWOOD planners were wrong.

Less than a fortnight after GOODWOOD (though for many quite literally a lifetime away!), another British attempt at armoured breakthrough would achieve a stunning success. On

30 July, the first day of Operation BLUECOAT, the Churchill tanks of 6th Guards Armoured Brigade left behind the infantry they were supposed to be supporting and plunged ahead into some of the densest bocage terrain of the *Suisse Normande* south of Caumont. In theory, this was not 'good tank country', but the worst possible terrain for tanks. In fact, in line with that very theory, the German defenders had felt they could economize on scarce antitank guns. The tanks achieved their breakthrough and were rejoined by their infantry before the stunned defenders could throw them back. As a modern observer has pointed out:

> *...ideal tank country is any area which lacks anti-tank weapons, i.e., it is better to attack across difficult terrain which is lightly held than across favourable ground which is strongly defended and where attack is expected.*[8]

With hindsight, one 3/RTR squadron commander recalls studying,

> *...some excellent photographs of all the villages and enemy positions in the line of our advance. Although we reckoned the countryside over which we were to advance seemed to be good tank country, and we were pleased to be away from the close bocage, it also proved to be good tank killing country.*[9]

And even with hindsight, ideas of 'good tank country' and even of mediaeval chivalry persisted, as in the 11th Armoured

'Although we reckoned the countryside over which we were to advance seemed to be good tank country... it also proved to be good tank killing country.' (A German Pak 40 guards the railway crossing west of Lirose.)

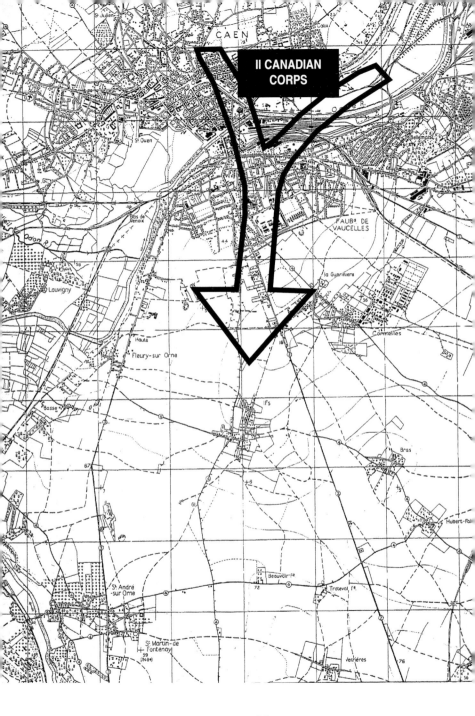

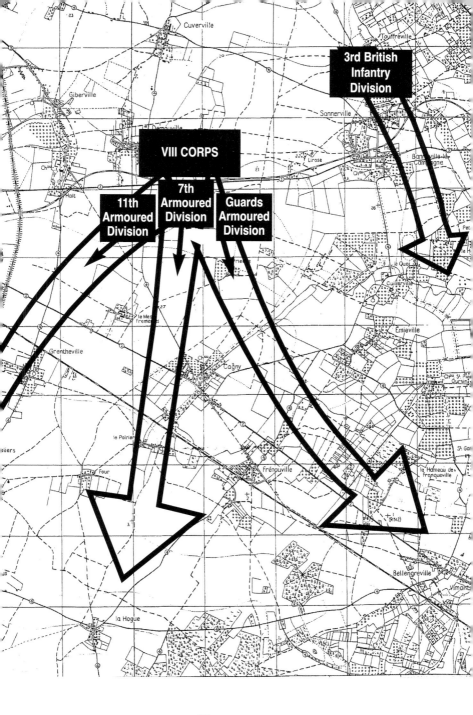

divisional history published in August, 1945:

> *To seek out the enemy's armour and destroy it'; the old slogan still sounded good. And if his champions kept to their tents, why then we must dare them to the fray, flaunting our panoply before their lines until for very shame they should come out and fight.*[10]

So the 'panoply' gathered ready for the flaunting. 'Pip' Roberts, commander of 11th Armoured, was later willing to admit the mistake:

> *We all came to the conclusion that if we had to operate it would be healthy to operate in the rolling country area south of Caen. And there we were, faced with an operation over that particular country. Of course the fact that the Germans appreciated that it was very good tank country too perhaps we did not consider too heavily.*[11]

References

1. *A Soldier's Story,* Omar Bradley, 1951, p 318.
2. Bradley, p 335-336.
3. Blumenson, p 188.
4. Bradley, p 341.
5. *Operations of Eighth Corps*, Lt Col G S Jackson, 1948, p 78.
6. Blumenson, p 190.
7. *Victory in the West*, L F Ellis, 1962, ISBN 1-870423-07-0, vol I, p 329.
8. *The Goodwood Concept,* Charles J Dick, Journal of the Royal United Services Institute, March 1982.
9. Close, p 115-116.
10. *Taurus Pursuant,* Edgar Palamountain, 1945, p 21.
11. Roberts, interview at Staff College, Camberley, 1979.

CHAPTER FIVE

THE ATTACKING FORCE

O'Connor's VIII Corps

The GOODWOOD plan was primarily a tank attack. All the supporting arms, including naval and air forces, were to play their part, but ultimately everything revolved around the three British armoured divisions present in Normandy. Without denying the importance of the other arms, it is the tanks and the tank men that will be examined most closely in this account.

The three armoured divisions, 7th, 11th and Guards, were brought together under General O'Connor's VIII Corps. This was very much a scratch formation. The Guards had not arrived in time to take part in VIII Corps' only previous battle, Operation EPSOM. 7th Armoured was 'borrowed' from XXX Corps, while the 15th (Scottish) Infantry Division was sent away under command of XII Corps. The Scottish division's General Macmillan was considerably annoyed at the disruption caused by the change and complained to his close friend O'Connor about 'corps flexibility at expense of identity'. O'Connor agreed, and loyal as ever to a hardly-done-by subordinate, he passed the message on. But his complaint brought from Montgomery a typically caustic response:

> You must understand that there is no such thing in my set-up as a permanent composition as a Corps; Divisions are grouped in Corps as the battle situation demands, and this is a great battle winning factor.

End of argument.

The Corps Commander, Major General Sir Richard O'Connor, had something to prove. His spectacular defeat of the Italian forces in northern Africa in 1941 had been followed by years as a prisoner of war in Italy. So it was that:

> The most fascinating of desert encounters – O'Connor versus Rommel – would never take place.[1]

After his escape, O'Connor was quickly given command of VIII Corps. But time had moved on. While he had fretted in prison, it fell to others to learn the tactical lessons of armoured warfare in the desert, especially in coming to terms with the vital role of

**Major General
Sir Richard
O'Connor.**

the antitank gun, which had accounted for three-quarters of British tank losses, and would do so again. Even O'Connor's sympathetic biographer concludes that from January, 1944, he 'lacked some of his original force and confidence.'[2] O'Connor was never especially favoured by Montgomery, who tended to believe his own propaganda that all his desert predecessors had been inefficient and unimaginative. What is more, when in February 1944, Montgomery decided to get rid of the Guards Armoured Division commander, General Adair, it was O'Connor who blocked the move. Sticking to his guiding principle of fairness towards subordinates, he refused to write the report critical of Adair requested by Montgomery's loyal deputy Dempsey (who had previously served under O'Connor). Remarkably for one marked by Montgomery for sacking, Adair stayed.

O'Connor's first Normandy battle, Operation EPSOM, had important consequences and can be judged a strategic success. But it had been an inglorious slogging match. What began as a promising advance to the sunny uplands beyond the Orne River came to a halt on the muddy banks of the Odon, and thereafter involved dogged defence instead of triumphant advances. Key decisions during the battle had been taken above the corps commander's head. O'Connor still had to prove himself.

The Armoured Divisions
Each of the three British armoured divisions that now made up O'Connor's VIII Corps was composed of an infantry brigade of

Sexton self-propelled 25-pounder.

three lorried ('motorized') battalions and an armoured brigade including three tank battalions plus a 'motor' battalion: armoured infantry mounted in tracked carriers and American half-tracks. Each division had two Royal Artillery field regiments of twenty-four 25-pounder field guns, one of the regiments towed behind 'Quad' prime movers and one of self-propelled 'Sextons', built on the chassis of Canadian 'Ram' tanks. The general assumption was that the towed artillery would support the infantry brigade and the SP regiment the armoured.

VIII Corps

Though similarly equipped the three divisions differed considerably in attitudes and leadership. 7th Armoured carried a reputation that was to prove a millstone. Much of the tactical experience the 'Desert Rats' had accumulated in the desert and scrublands of the North Africa campaign proved unhelpful in the dense countryside of Normandy. As a bombardier in the division's attached antitank regiment (the Norfolk Yeomanry) recalled:

> *The chaps who had been in the desert detested Normandy and Europe. You could not see a thing half the time, and you were just sitting tight, I suppose the whole Division felt the same. In the desert we could see them but not knock them out, with the 2-pdrs anyway; in Europe we could knock them out but not see them. I think round Caen was the worst of all, we were getting mortared and shelled for days without anything to get back at.*[3]

Old soldiers had to learn new tricks. Morale was not helped by the disaster at Villers-Bocage, and although this was followed by a creditable performance later in June, Dempsey was later to claim,

> *My feeling that Bucknall* [XXX Corps] *and Erskine* [7th Armoured] *would have to go started with that failure. By this time 7th Armoured Division was living on its reputation and the whole handling of that battle was a disgrace.*

Things were to get worse before they got better. After GOODWOOD, desertion rates increased and only after Erskine's sacking and the redeployment of a hundred officers, veterans of 8th Army days, was the situation stabilized.

Guards Armoured Division had not yet seen combat, and had something to prove. Some maintained that aristocratic Guards officers would be familiar with motor cars, and therefore at home in tanks. Others had opposed the very idea of forming an armoured unit from the Brigade of Guards, and indeed it was to infantry that the Guards reverted as soon as the war was over. This was perhaps for the best.

For all the strength of their tradition and unquestioned enthusiasm, Guards Armoured arrived in Normandy woefully ill-equipped to learn the lessons of combined arms tactics. In fairness, much of the pre-invasion training given to the British army focused on weapons skills rather than battlefield tactics. The form and content of training was largely a regimental matter, with little central direction or 'filtering down' of known German tactics from central intelligence to units in the field. But Guards Armoured seems to have been particularly resistant to new ideas. Early in 1944, a senior Coldstream Guards officer commented that 'if the Guards had ever learned sub-unit fire and movement, they had since forgotten it,' while the Guards' commander General Adair expressed contentment with an exercise which had turned into 'a tank gallop through the best of the hunting country near Towcester'.[4] As a Royal Artillery battery commander with Guards Armoured through the Normandy campaign recalled,

> *I never saw infantry and armour working together in England. The infantry brigade and the armoured brigade were expected to operate separately, and I do not think that my own division was ready for the shock of reality of 18 July, although the 11th Armoured had already been through the fire on Point 112.*[5]

As a result of decisions made at the Casablanca conference, 11th Armoured Division narrowly missed being sent to Tunisia, where by 1943 the need was for infantry rather than more

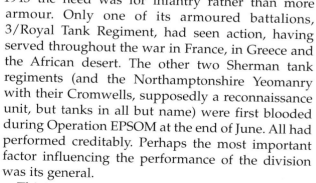

armour. Only one of its armoured battalions, 3/Royal Tank Regiment, had seen action, having served throughout the war in France, in Greece and the African desert. The other two Sherman tank regiments (and the Northamptonshire Yeomanry with their Cromwells, supposedly a reconnaissance unit, but tanks in all but name) were first blooded during Operation EPSOM at the end of June. All had performed creditably. Perhaps the most important factor influencing the performance of the division was its general.

Thirty-seven years old, the 11th Armoured Division's Major General 'Pip' Roberts was the

Major General 'Pip' Roberts

youngest British divisional commander. He had fought in tanks throughout the North Africa campaign, and had learned tank tactics in the hard school of desert combat. 'Pip' Roberts was a desert fighter who was nevertheless able to learn the different tactics needed to succeed in Normandy. Though the first to admit the shortcomings of the pre-invasion training ('exercises, even as realistic as Exercise EAGLE had been, cannot really test men for battle'), nevertheless 11th Armoured did practice the rudiments of tank-infantry co-operation on which they were to build substantially in Normandy. This was to lead to friction with Corps Commander O'Connor.

Roberts and O'Connor

In 11th Armoured Division's first battle, Operation EPSOM, O'Connor took a very 'hands on' approach. At an early stage, he ordered the division's armoured brigade to support the infantry of 15th Scottish, leading one officer in the armoured division's own infantry brigade to observe,

> ...we might well have wondered to what purpose we had spent the last three years training ourselves in close armoured/infantry co-operation if we were immediately to be separated from each other in our first battle.[6]

O'Connor had something to prove. By early afternoon of the first day, O'Connor felt that the Scots had broken through the main German line and ordered Roberts to release his tanks, like the cavalry of old in pursuit of a broken enemy. Roberts realized that O'Connor had mis-read the situation, as was proved when his tanks were fought to a standstill on Hill 112. In the days that followed, Roberts showed an independent streak. Denied permission to sack a senior officer, he went over the heads of both O'Connor and Dempsey, gaining the permission he needed from Montgomery himself (Monty, like Roberts, applauded youthful vigour and determination in his officers). Conflict with O'Connor was to become more problematic with GOODWOOD.

The planners of Operation GOODWOOD had few opportunities for inspired creativity. The key challenges were the sheer logistics of getting three armoured divisions across parallel waterways, turning them through ninety degrees, and funnelling them down a narrow avenue of advance. By necessity, the GOODWOOD orders were constraining, dominated by timekeeping and strictly choreographed vehicle movements. As O'Connor's biographer put it,

> *O'Connor and his staff were perhaps more concerned with the mechanics of 'GOODWOOD' than with the philosophy of it.*[7]

VIII Corps' planning staff appeared to be descending to micro-management of the Operation, and the divisional commanders were understandably not pleased.

On paper, the plan seemed reasonable enough. Preceded by a massive aerial bombardment to crack open the enemy lines, 11th Armoured would break in, then secure the right flank by seizing Bras and Rocquancourt, atop the Bourguébus ridge and astride the main Caen-Falaise road. Guards Armoured would follow closely, securing Cagny on the right flank and pushing further east towards Vimont to stretch wider the hole in the German lines. Then, 7th Armoured would burst through the centre, over the Bourguébus ridge to establish on the village of St-Aignan-de-Cramesnil. Indeed, it was not the basic philosophy of the plan to which Roberts objected. His concern was that his division was required not only to break into and through the German lines, but also to capture various strongpoints along the way, an entirely different proposition.

Roberts' initial orders were to secure the villages of Cuverville and Démouville on the right and Cagny on the left.

> *I didn't care for this very much because to take Cuverville and Démouville was clearly a two Battalion operation, and then to do that I should have to leave an artillery regiment which normally worked with the infantry brigade, and I would also have to give them some tank support. So right at the outset, I was going to be minus almost half the division. a severe handicap to my further operations. As it were, with one hand behind my back. In addition, I had been given Cagny, and I thought that would delay our advance.*[8]

Never shy of stating his case, Roberts remonstrated with O'Connor, first to his face and then in writing. Why could not 51st Highland Division, already in the front line, take on these tasks? O'Connor was not empowered to permit this. Unknown to Roberts, Montgomery was not only dissatisfied with the performance of the 51st, but was also adamant that substantial infantry forces be kept in reserve to guard against unforeseeable reverses. O'Connor stood his ground, albeit with one concession.

The corps commander wouldn't agree to relieve me of the first requirement... I finally was told that if I didn't feel it was a sound plan... then he would get another armoured division to lead. But there was one amelioration, and that was that instead of having to 'take' Cagny, I was only required to 'mask' it.[9]

Roberts bowed to the inevitable, agreeing effectively to fight the battle without his motorized infantry brigade and their artillery. Even more important to the outcome of the battle, as it was to turn out, was his determination not to get involved with Cagny.

The Weapons

11th and Guards Armoured Divisions were principally equipped with the American Sherman tank, a 'medium' tank of about thirty tons. The Sherman was designed to the American philosophy that tanks were weapons of exploitation, most effective when rampaging around an enemy's rear areas following a breakthrough. The Sherman tank was not initially intended to fight enemy tanks. That was the task of 'tank destroyers', specialist towed or self-propelled antitank guns, which unlike British antitank units (whose doctrine was essentially defensive) were intended aggressively to seek out their prey. The standard Sherman tank used at GOODWOOD carried a dual-purpose, medium velocity 75mm gun with a

Captured Panther on a British 40 ton tank transporter, designed to move the Churchill tank. Note the overhanging tracks of the Panther.

1. M10 'Achilles' self-propelled 17-pounder.

2. The standard British Sherman 5 (American M4A4).

3. Sherman 5C the 17-pounder 'Firefly'.

most effective High Explosive round, and an Armour Piercing round with relatively poor penetrative capability.

Unlike the Americans, the British recognized in the months before invasion that the armoured divisions needed to be better prepared for the possibility of tank-vs-tank combat. To this end, each Royal Artillery antitank regiment assigned to an armoured division exchanged one or two of its four batteries of towed 17-pounder guns for self-propelled M10 carriages. These were based on tank chassis, with open-topped turrets carrying either a three-inch high velocity gun ('Wolverines') or an even more effective 17-pounder ('Achilles'). (This arrangement was viewed as a temporary expedient for the early stages of invasion, but in the end was left in place.) Additionally, as more 17-pounder tubes became available, an innovative British designer managed to fit the gun into a Sherman turret. The result was the Sherman 'Firefly'. Supplied to the regiments on a ratio of one Firefly to three 75mm Sherman or Cromwell tanks, the Firefly was most often allocated with one per four-tank troop.

The Firefly made a difference. Equipped with one of these, a

British troop of four tanks gained at least the possibility of penetrating the frontal armour of a German Mark V (*Panther*) or Mark VI (*Tiger*). It was not infallible. Early in July, the 23/Hussars:

> *...were anxious to see what effect a Sherman would have on the front of a Panther, should we find ourselves in the unfortunate position of having to tackle one, or more, frontally.*

In a trial shoot against a *Panther* knocked out by the 24/Lancers near Rauray,

> *It was found that a 75 millimetre gun made no impression on the front at all, unless it was lucky enough to hit the turret ring, a very small target indeed. The 17-pounder was more encouraging... for it penetrated the front of the Panther's turret at three hundred yards, though it did not always go through the sloped front plate of the hull.*

The Hussars concluded '...that head-on Panthers should be treated with circumspection', and in combat a few days later results were to prove 'just as unhappy as our trial shoot indicated.'[10]

As experience accumulated, it was recognized that the Firefly's distinctive long gun made it a prime target for German gunners, and increasingly it came to be used in 'overwatch', lingering behind the other three tanks of the troop to give covering fire when enemy armour was revealed. Though in some instances the 'lingering' was rather further back than the advancing elements of the troop would have wished! (Note that the term 'Firefly' was often – though not uniformly – used for any vehicle carrying a 17-pounder gun.) The armour penetration of this excellent gun was further enhanced by use of the new 'Armour Piercing, Discarding Sabot' round: a slim, heavy dart encased in a 'sabot' which filled out the 76mm bore of the gun. On firing, the sabot fell away but the projectile retained the enhanced kinetic energy imparted by the larger bore. O'Connor pressed his Army commander so hard on the issue of 17-pounders, that Dempsey was compelled in late June to promise to VIII Corps:

> *17-pounders in all forms and SABOT ammunition are absolutely first in our priority for equipment. The QMG and all those concerned are quite clear about this.*[11]

So great was the success of the Firefly that American tank units cried out for similar equipment. Even when a new, 76mm

Sherman tank gun became available, the penetrative capability of its Armour Piercing round was not a dramatic improvement over the 75mm, and its High Explosive round was actually inferior. Eisenhower famously to bemoaned,

> *You mean our 76 won't knock these Panthers out? Why is it that I am always the last to hear about this stuff. Ordnance told me this 76 would take care of anything the German had. Now I find you can't knock out a damn thing with it.*[12]

The 17-pounder gun was offered to the Americans; Montgomery was keen that they should adopt it.[13] But as late as August, 1944, the US Ordnance department was refusing to release M4 Sherman tanks for conversion[14], and as the war entered a new and more mobile phase, the project was dropped.

The third armoured division to take the stage for GOODWOOD was equipped differently. In place of Shermans, 7th Armoured Division had British Cromwell tanks. Descended from a line of British-designed 'cruiser' tanks whose performance varied from barely battleworthy to downright appalling, the Cromwell was to prove one of the more successful British designs of the war. Compared to the Sherman, the Cromwell was acceptable in most respects and even superior in some. It had a good turn of speed, it was reliable, and its main gun proved especially responsive in laying and firing. But the favourable comparison counted for little. Just as the Sherman was no match for 1944-vintage German battle tanks, neither was the Cromwell. Like its sister tank divisions in VIII Corps, 7th Armoured also enhanced the firepower of its

The Cromwell had a good turn of speed.

four-tank troops with a Sherman 17-pounder Firefly alongside the three Cromwells. One disadvantage of the Cromwell, especially in the Normandy campaign, was its unfamiliarity and, from a distance, its passing resemblance to the most commonly encountered German tank, the *Panzer IV*. Arriving in Normandy, 2/Northants Yeomanry lost no time in circulating details of their tanks' appearance to neighbouring units. As one of their number recalled:

> Our own troops seemed only to know Sherman and Churchill tanks and would often mistake Cromwells for Germans.[15]

'Friendly fire' incidents occurred. Weeks later, in their first action, a Coldstream Guards Sherman spotted a potential enemy and there ensued:

> ...a long argument as to whom it belonged. No one could tell and we were ready to shoot when it turned and could be identified as ours, a Welsh Guards Cromwell.[16]

As well as the 'sabre' squadrons of 7th Armoured, Cromwell tanks were also to be found in the reconnaissance regiments of each of the armoured divisions: 2/Northants Yeomanry in 11th Armoured; 2/Welsh Guards in Guards Armoured; and 8/Hussars in 7th Armoured (this latter only differentiated from its fellow Cromwell-equipped tank regiments by its lack of Fireflies). Although each armoured division normally had an armoured car regiment attached for forward reconnaissance, the thinking was that something with more firepower was needed in 1944. The thinking was sound; the solution was not. Had the Allied armies of 1944 possessed a truly 'heavy' tank, then something lighter and faster for reconnaissance would have been an excellent idea. But given the Sherman as the main battle tank of the day, it was rather pointless to pretend that the Cromwell – marginally more agile but essentially of equivalent performance – should be employed differently. GOODWOOD was to reveal the fallacy of the Cromwell reconnaissance regiment theory.

Another questionable approach to reconnaissance was to be found within each of the nine British armoured regiments taking the stage at GOODWOOD. Each of these had its own reconnaissance squadron, made up of wheeled scout cars and a dozen American 'Stuart' tanks. This light tank's predecessors had won a reputation for reliability in the desert, where its shortcomings had been forgiven and its relatively good

A Guards' Armoured 'Honey', still with its turret.

reliability earned it the name 'Honey' by which it would be known to the British throughout the war. But by 1944 even the later models of the *Honey* were obsolete and widely reviled by their crews. The recce troop of the Inniskillings (of 7th Armoured) had been overjoyed to receive Cromwell tanks similar to those of the sabre squadrons, at the same time that Army Order upgraded them from a recce 'troop' to a 'squadron'. But soon came disappointment.

The Recce Squadron had a nasty shock. It took the form of the light 'Stuart' tank... this atrocity on tracks. The gunners who fired the 37mm cannon... found it accurate enough, but thought little of its chances against anything tougher than a water truck.[17]

The 23/Hussars' Recce Squadron (of 11th Armoured) had already converted from Carriers to Crusader tanks before being converted yet again to Stuarts, and the change was unwelcome. The Stuart,

...carried a 37-millimetre gun but for reconnaissance purposes had the disadvantage of standing too high. They were thus difficult to conceal.[18]

Apart from its height and small gun, the Stuart suffered from a very cramped turret. This problem was exacerbated in later models by the addition of a turret 'basket' – effectively, a suspended turret floor. In the desert, the British had tended to avoid rotating the Stuart turret at all for fear of upsetting arrangements within the turret (Stuart tank commanders fought standing on the padded central drive shaft). Later in the European campaign (as the Americans began to replace their Stuarts with the superior M24 Chaffee) the British answer to the new turret basket was to remove the turret altogether. Especially in reconnaissance units, the conspicuous turret was regarded as more a liability than an asset. Some Stuarts on the GOODWOOD battlefield had already undergone this transformation, including the Reconnaissance Troop of 3/RTR and half the Troop of 23/Hussars, also the 'sawn-off Honeys' of Royal Artillery officers who, as ever in an advance, were not with their batteries but forward with the units their guns were supporting. But with or without its 37mm peashooter, the Stuarts served on the GOODWOOD battlefield as a relatively small target attracting enemy fire which might otherwise have been directed at more valuable tanks. Typically at the front of any advance, few survived GOODWOOD unscathed.

In the British Army, such field modifications were not uncommon. Even before their first action in Normandy, many British Sherman tank units had already discarded the external .50 calibre Browning machine gun thoughtfully provided by the American manufacturers for anti-aircraft defence. Though a potent weapon, these externally mounted guns tended to snag trees, to increase the visibility of an already high-profile tank, and crucially required the operator to be exposed at a time when – rumour had it – even fingers exposed on the hatch rim risked being picked off by German snipers. Other changes were tried by the Fife and Forfars. Steel Brownlie relates that:

> Some boffin hit on the idea of welding extra armour to protect the [ammunition] bins, but their only effect, so far as I could see, was to provide an aiming mark. I certainly saw many brewed-up Shermans with a neat hole in the 'extra armour'.[19]

And in Jack Thorpe's tank, the morning of 11 July was spent,

> ...removing the perforated iron cage round the lower part of the revolving turret basket with hammers and chisels (bad design, not made for battle, the cage may prevent an empty shell case jettisoned from the gun breech from being projected at us sitting in the 'engine' cockpit, but it would prevent our escape in the event of our having to climb out through the turret with the gun turned to seal the drivers' hatches).[20]

And the Northamptonshire Yeomanry went to great trouble to cover the external surfaces of their Cromwell tanks with glued-on strips of rubber, as a deterrent to German magnetic mines.

Bluddy Cauld Smelly Contraptions

GOODWOOD is remembered as a battle of tanks, but of course tanks were crewed by men. Sitting today inside a stripped-out Sherman tank is an uncomfortable experience, not recommended for anyone liable to claustrophobia. Disregarding the engine to the rear and the transmission at the very front, the crew space of a Sherman is an armoured box barely greater than that in a modern off-road car. And there the resemblance ends.

Over the front of that windowless metal box clambered the driver (on the left; this was an American-built tank) and co-driver, through their separate forward hatches. Once inside, the driver squeezed into his seat between dual steering columns, the co-driver behind the breech of his .30 calibre Browning machine gun. The three-man turret crew entered through the single hatch on the very top of the turret. First through the narrow hatch, the loader-wireless operator ducked under the breech of the 75mm gun to take his place on the turret floor to the left of the gun. Next to climb in, the gunner squirmed into his seat, forward to the right of the gun, hands on elevation and traverse controls, foot on the floor triggers. Necessarily last in and usually first out, the commander perched with his head hovering half out of the open hatch, his eyes level with the coaming, and his right leg almost touching the gunner (so close that a nudge of the knee might replace or reinforce an intercom command).

This being a fighting vehicle, the crew shared the restricted and dimly lit space with an array of weaponry. This included: two .30 calibre machine guns and their 6,000 rounds contained in twenty-five ammunition tins (the belts loaded in varying sequences of Armour Piercing, tracer, and ball); a smoke mortar mounted in the turret roof with three 'ready' rounds alongside and six more in boxes; a Bren gun, a Thompson sub-machine gun, and a Sten gun, all with their ammunition clips; a signal flare pistol and its cartridges; and an assortment of mixed hand grenades (fragmentation, white phosphorous, and coloured

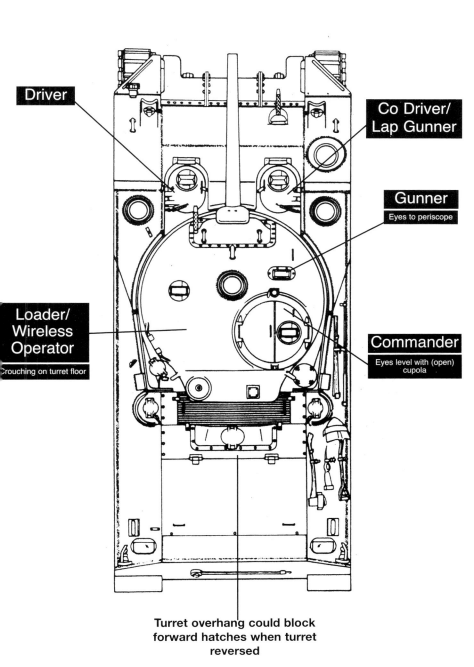

Driver

Co Driver/ Lap Gunner

Gunner
Eyes to periscope

Loader/ Wireless Operator
Crouching on turret floor

Commander
Eyes level with (open) cupola

Turret overhang could block
forward hatches when turret
reversed

smoke). Plus of course the 75mm main gun whose breech and protective recoil screens divided the turret in two and whose seventy or more rounds (sometimes as many as a hundred, split between Armour Piecing, High Explosive, and smoke) filled every remaining space within the loader's reach. In a 'Firefly,' the bigger 17-pounder gun took up so much space that the co-driver's position had to be replaced with ammunition racks.

The layout of a Cromwell tank was similar, though as it was British the interior layout was reversed to allow right hand drive (ironically, as it was destined to fight mostly in lands where the rule of the road was to drive on the right!). It was marginally more cramped.

The Cromwell tank is not comfortable to live in. For one thing hardly any movement is possible inside it, and for another it is nearly always very cold, as air for the engine is drawn through the turret and a gale comes in at the driver's open visor.

However,

It carried not only discomfort for the enemy, but rations and bedding those whose home it was for so long, and many became greatly attached to their tanks by the end of the war.[21]

For the tank was not simply a fighting vehicle. After long debate the British government finally in mid-1943 allowed the fertile Yorkshire Wolds to be chewed up by tank tracks. There, in the great Exercises culminating in EAGLE, tank crews began to become accustomed to living in their tanks, day-in and day-out. Somewhere amongst all the instruments of death, room was found for sleeping bags and greatcoats (invariably lost or shredded by shell splinters if left outside the armour plate), shaving and mess kits, food and water, and small personal 'luxuries': a pipe, a book, perhaps even a forbidden diary.

All our tanks were personalized in various ways, so that you could lay your hand on anything, without thinking.

One 2/Fife and Forfar wireless operator was wounded on 15 July.

He was badly hurt but did not complain, and, before he was taken away, he quietly asked one of us to go and get a book he had been reading from alongside the wireless set in his turret.[22]

Another operator, in 3/RTR, was wounded in the legs during GOODWOOD. Finding the rest of his crew dead, the commander set about rescuing the crippled operator.

The first thing he said was, 'Have you brought the cigarettes,

Sarge?' I replied, 'Which cigarettes?' 'Those in the haversack,' was the reply.[23]

The first thought of the wounded trooper was for the treasured possessions he had left behind in his mobile 'home' (he received instead a dose of morphine, the badly burned sergeant then carrying him back four miles before himself collapsing at the Field Dressing Station).

Every three days, the Quartermaster's truck would pass down the lines flinging out boxes of 'Compo' rations, each marked 'A', 'B', 'C', etc., indicating different menus, and crews would scramble to select their favourite. Each box contained a day's rations for fourteen men, so the five-man tank crews understandably felt short-changed. (In a Firefly with its four-man crew the Compo rations stretched further, though the workload was correspondingly higher.) Some of the tins of food contained more than five helpings, and were hard to eke out over three days. Tins of meat would be wedged under a hot exhaust pipe to warm up during the day, while the hard-tack biscuits, jam, and processed cheese would be kept handy (by the wireless set or in the co-driver's compartment) to keep hunger at bay during the day. If the ration of toilet paper was less than

Sherman tank crew outside their 'mobile home'.

A near miss on a Sherman. Snipers and artillery took their toll of 'head up' tank commanders.

generous, at something under three sheets per man per day, most acknowledged that the food was adequate. 'It was basic, but nobody went hungry.'[24]

One Scot complained that 'Naebody but a man could live in a bluddy cauld, smelly contraption lik yin o' thae things'.

The armour was far from waterproof; rain poured in through open hatches, and every aperture attracted dust since the engine sucked its air in through the crew compartment. In action, this might be a relief as extractor fans struggled to clear the hot accumulation of fumes from cordite, sweat, and the empty shell cases which were passed around as the only means of sanitation. And always there was the knowledge that the protective armour enclosed not only men and explosives in close proximity, but to either side were fuel tanks containing up to eighty gallons of combustible petrol. The tankers' home was a travelling bomb. Still, home it became.

Tankers wrote of their good fortune to be able to carry their provisions and small luxuries around with them, free of the infantryman's fear of theft or of the 'Echelon' trucks failing to make it forward at the end of the day. Men worked out complicated arrangements for sleeping entirely within the tank. As co-driver, Jack Thorpe included in his duties the role of cook, and prided himself on his recipe for cups of 'char' which disguised the taste of the optimistically-labelled packets of 'tea powder' and the chloride of lime in the drinking water. He learned (wholly illegally) to brew up on the move.

> I removed the upholstered seat and put the stove on the seat frame and set about boiling the water, holding the dixie on and taking up the shocks and the lurching motion. It got a bit dicey at times when the water was nearly boiling and slurping up and over the sides. Still... it was very much appreciated.[25]

Somehow, most men stood the strain. Some cracked. Diaries casually refer to nervous breakdowns: 'once they had left us... we did not hear from them again';[26] others to self-inflicted wounds. One such case, after several unproductive attempts at falling off his tank,

> ...getting desperate, knowing we should be moving up into action in an hour or so, he did the positive thing of lifting up the heavy engine hatch, placing his one hand inside and dropping the hatch. He was evacuated... It was a nervous, testing time for us all.

For one tank sergeant, a German shell spraying muck over a newly-served feast of tinned potatoes and McConachie's stew was the last straw:

> The Sergeant blows his top, cracks up and is completely off his head, runs this way and that, shouting and screaming and blubbering. His crew go after him and eventually hold him down in a ditch, but he is berserk, jumping about and punching... until they finally tie him up with pack straps for his own safety... Just another casualty - but this time to the mind.[27]

Steel Brownlie,

> ...gave my Firefly commander a bollocking for not keeping up. He exploded that no one had called him a coward before, but I ignored that and walked away. Hearing a scuffle, I turned to see Tpr Cross grappling with him. He had his loaded pistol in his hand, and evidently intended to shoot me in the back.[28]

The young troop leader took no action against the old desert hand, who subsequently behaved well.

On the morning of 18 July, a Fife and Forfar trooper was sitting at the bow machine gun when,

> *Suddenly over the intercom I got the message, 'Hull gunner. Target in front. Forty yards, four-oh yards. FIRE!'*

I snatched my gun and applied my eyes to the periscope but I saw only a solitary khaki clad figure... it was Captain Leith. I picked up the microphone and yelled at Pat, 'What the hell do you mean?'

> *'FIRE!'* shouted Pat.

'Get into the gunner's seat and fire yourself!' I yelled back at Pat.

> *'You're on a charge,'* snarls Pat.

'Balls,' I replied, *'You couldn't make it stick.'*

> *I do not think Pat was kidding* [but] *it was soonest forgotten; we remained good friends.*[29]

Prior to GOODWOOD, the attitudes of the three armoured divisions' tank crews were somewhat different. Himself an expert in tank warfare, 'Pip' Roberts was well placed to observe these differences in a post-war interview. As to the Guards, 'As far as I knew, nobody in the division had fought in armour before.' However,

> *They had a view on the battle very much the same as ours* [in 11th Armoured]*: they were raring to go and show what they could do.*

7th Armoured, which Roberts knew well,

> *...were quite different... They had come back* [from Africa] *just in time for Christmas and had some nice leave, and were I think, with so much experience, a little too wary (wary, not weary!) and a little too canny. And they certainly did not have the same enthusiasm for this battle as ourselves and Guards Armoured Division.*

As to 11th Armoured, Roberts naturally praised the three tank regiments who had served him so well in Europe, though interestingly he contrasted the relative inexperience of 23/Hussars and 2/Fife and Forfar Yeomanry with the old desert hands of 3/Royal Tank Regiment, and not entirely to the credit of 3/RTR. Their greater experience had also made them 'canny'; they had to be well led in order to

> *...hold their end up with the tremendous élan which the other, new, fresh regiments were producing.*[30]

The wonder is that so many of these tank crews were able to endure for so long such inhuman conditions. This was largely due to team spirit. Psychologists have long recognized that most soldiers' primary loyalty is to their closest comrades in arms: the section or even the squad. In some units, loyalty to a higher formation may be a factor, but 'looking out for your mates' generally comes first. In a tank, this bond became stronger still.

In action, every man had a strenuous job to do: the driver endlessly pumping the clutches and hauling on the steering rods, the loader nimbly dodging the moving gun while lifting heavy shells from their stowage into the breech, the gunner with forehead pressed tight to brow-pad peering through a narrow telescope ready to hit a distant target before it responded in like manner. Each man knew that his survival was dependent on himself and his mates carrying out their individual tasks, responding without question to commands over the intercom. Few had a clear idea of what was happening. The gunner's field of vision was a narrow telescopic sight; the driver's little better, and sometimes non-existent when dust obscured his view. Of all the crew, only the loader-operator at his radio and the commander in his open hatch had much idea of the tactical situation, and they were usually too busy with their own multiple tasks to have time to reflect on the 'big picture'.

During the long summer days of the Normandy campaign all crewmen were more-or-less numbed by lack of sleep, or else by the Benzedrine pills issued to keep them awake; in action their instinctive fear was somewhat offset by natural adrenaline. The

A Sherman passes two knocked out *panzer* **Mk IVs.**

crews formed strong bonds.

A tank crew is something special. They don't choose their companions, but it becomes a close-knit unit who are all enclosed together in a close confined proximity inside their tank and have no privacy. Sometimes for days and weeks they live together working as a team.[31]

More prosaically, an officer of the Sherwood Rangers commented, 'Tank crews which fell out with each other were much more likely to end up dead.'[32]

References

1. *The Desert Generals,* Correlli Barnet, 1960, p 63.
2. *The Forgotten Victor,* John Baynes, 1989, ISBN 0-08-036269-9, p 183.
3. *The Norfolk Yeomanry,* Jeremy Bastin, 1986, ISBN 0-95111664-0-9, p 229.
4. *Military Training in the British Army,* Timothy Harrison Place, 2000, ISBN 0-7146-5037-4, p 121 and 108.
5. *Against Odds,* Dominick Graham, 1999, ISBN 0-333-66859-6, p 133 & 170.
6. *The 4th KSLI in Normandy,* Major 'Ned' Thornburn, 1990, p 21.
7. Baynes, p 201.
8. Roberts, interview at Staff College, Camberley, 1979.
9. Roberts, interview at Staff College, Camberley, 1979.
10. *The Story of the 23rd Hussars,* Geoffrey Bishop, 1946, p 67.
11. Jackson, p 26.
12. Bradley, p 322-323.
13. *The Universal Tank,* David Fletcher, 1993, ISBN 0 11 290534 X, p 102..
14. Memorandum by Brigadier General Holly, USA A FV & W Section, 9 August 1944.
15. Interview Corporal R J Spittles, 2nd Northamptonshire Yeomanry.
16. *Armoured Guardsman,* Robert Boscawen, 2001, ISBN 0 85052 748 1, p 32.
17. *First In Last Out,* Corporal John Pilborough, 1986.
18. Bishop, p 27.
19. *And Came Safe Home* (Diary), W Steel Brownlie.
20. *A Soldier's Tale* (Diary), Trooper John Thorpe, 1982 and 1987.
21. *Welsh Guards at War,* L F Ellis, 1946, p 38.
22. Steel Brownlie, diary.
23. Jim Caswell, diary.
24. Steel Brownlie, diary.
25. Thorpe, diary.
26. Steel Brownlie, diary.
27. Thorpe, diary.
28. Steel Brownlie, diary.
29. Thorpe, diary.
30. Roberts, interview at Staff College, Camberley, 1979.
31. Thorpe diary.
32. *By Tank into Normandy,* Stuart Hills, 2002, ISBN 0-304-36216-6, p 99.

CHAPTER SIX

THE DEFENDERS

The Failure of German Intelligence

It is a tribute to the resilience of the German army that its Normandy front still held so firmly in mid-July. *Generalfeldmarschall* Erwin Rommel despaired at Hitler's continuing refusal to consider the withdrawal of forces out of naval artillery range to a more practical defensive line, if not the Siegfried Line on the borders of the Fatherland, at least to the river Seine. Meanwhile, the *Führerhauptquartier* still resisted the release of considerable forces from the coastal areas of northern France, insisting that there remained a threat of further invasion from England.

In fact, this threat was non-existent. Neither the air and naval lift capability nor suitably trained ground forces for a further invasion existed. General Eisenhower clearly indicated that 'sideshow excursions' were not going to be allowed to dissipate the main effort through the existing beachhead, and the last

Erwin Rommel's plan depended on stopping the invasion on the beaches.

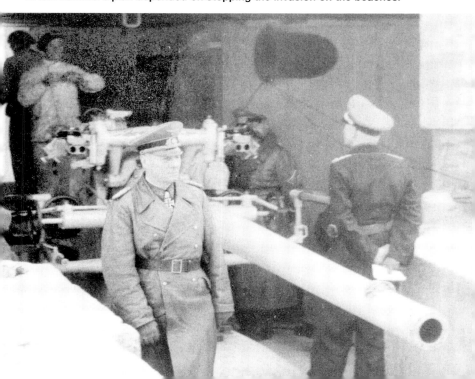

amphibious assault-trained division (the American 28th Infantry) was released from reserve on 13 July to be deployed in the field.[1] In part, the Germans were deceived by a brilliantly executed programme of deception involving fictitious military units in England and misleading radio transmissions, and not least by the 'turning' of the few spies still operating on the British mainland. Also, the Germans were guilty of self-delusion. As Hitler came to pin more and more of his hopes on the impact of the 'V' weapons programme, fears correspondingly grew that the V1 launch sites would be a likely invasion target. The commander of a *Panzer* division still held north of the Seine *(116. PzDiv.)* wrote on 24 June:

> *Bombs are falling everywhere. They seem to be desperately searching for the positions of the V-1s, which are apparently very bothersome to them.*[2]

These delusions were given added weight by two sources: *Fremde-Heer-West*, the department of intelligence charged with estimating enemy resources; and the *Abwehr,* German counter-intelligence. Both supported fears of a further invasion. Prior to the June landings, with more and more force at risk of being withdrawn from the defence of the west in order to feed the insatiable needs of the Russian front, each department had grossly overestimated the quantity of Allied troops available in England, by as many as thirty divisions. Now that the invasion was a reality, and those fictitious Allied divisions had failed to materialize in Normandy, both agencies were understandably reluctant to admit the deception to the *Führer*. The Allied deception plan lent substance to the mythical divisions as a force in being, just waiting to descend on the coast between the Seine and Somme rivers. It seems barely credible that, on the eve of GOODWOOD, serious thought was being given to moving the élite *12. SS-Panzerdivision* north away from Normandy, but, in fact, movement orders were being issued as late as 16 July. Such a move was bound to inspire conspiracy theories. Was there was indeed a plot between Rommel, Speidel, and von Kluge to remove this *'Führertreu'* [loyal] unit from the area, immediately before the Hitler assassination attempt of 20 July, in preparation for a *Wehrmacht* led truce with the Allies in Normandy? Or did Rommel truly believe in the possibility of further invasion? We may never know.

The War of Logistics

German small unit tactics won the admiration of their opponents during the Second World War and have since been studied and emulated by modern armies. By contrast, it is increasingly clear that the provisioning of their ground forces was a major German weakness. One recent study concludes that the German army *'consistently neglected logistics in preference to their concentration on tactical excellence.'*[3] The battle of Normandy can be regarded as a large-scale meeting engagement, in which the first side to reinforce the forward positions would hold the advantage. From the day that three airborne and five amphibious divisions first overcame the coastal defences of Normandy, a race began with each side striving to build up force in the new theatre faster than the enemy. The Allies had to cope with a sea crossing beset by tides and storms, the Germans with enemy command of the air.

Both sides experienced crises. For the Allies, the inability to supply enough 'POL' (petrol, oil, and lubricants, the lifeblood of a mobile army) was to become critical in August. Few had dared rely on 'PLUTO', the untried experiment of laying a bulk fuel 'Pipe Line Under The Ocean' from the Isle of White to Cherbourg. But without it the Allies' prosecution of the war in France might well by Autumn have stopped dead in its tracks.

The Germans' crisis began even before the invasion. Rommel's 'Atlantic Wall' strategy set out to stop the invasion on the beaches, before it could establish a lodgement. German sources reveal that the plan required upwards of fifty million landmines. Between February and June, only four million were laid. Allied air power simply made impossible the delivery by rail of sufficient mines from the massive stores far away in Verdun.[4] The

A 'Teller' plate-mine on a stake.

same was true in other fields. The Germans depended on French ammunition stores which were typically inland, far from the front. Storage facilities nearer the front were inadequate, making units dependent on 'hand-to-mouth' delivery, most often relying on rail transport right up to the war zone. Given the railways' vulnerability to air attack, for as much as

63

seventeen hours out of twenty-four during the long summer days, adequate distribution of vital supplies was never achieved. Civilian vehicles, bicycles, and horses were seized – 7th Army alone had 45,000 horses in Normandy – but could not fill the needs of its sixteen divisions (eight of which were officially 'static'). The mobile divisions in turn were forced to donate many of their transport vehicles into a common supply pool and, consequently their own mobility suffered. On numerous occasions, the redeployment of vital *Panzer* divisions was slowed by lack of fuel. Even the élite units were affected: ULTRA decryption of an 11 July report by 2. SS-*Panzerdivision* revealed that shortages of fuel and most types of ammunition had resulted in the loss of twenty-two tanks, seven guns, and seven lorries.[5] On 10 July alone, in the Caen sector, the Allies expended 80,000 artillery shells; in reply the German could only manage 4,500. Mere days before the invasion, Berlin had ordered that one hundred million rifle rounds be sent from France to the Russian front. Throughout the Normandy campaign, there are reports of German infantry and even tanks having to resort to firing wooden practice bullets. A full fifty per cent of German *Eihandgranate* in Normandy were unused due to lack of fuzes.[6] Well might a senior German protest that, 'Although our troop morale is good, we cannot meet the enemy matériel with courage alone.'[7]

The Failure of Allied Intelligence

In spite of almost total command of the daytime skies over Normandy, Allied intelligence had a less than perfect appreciation of the German defences south-east of Caen. For a variety of reasons, the first half of July was a very lean time for ULTRA decrypts. Army patrols brought in prisoners for interrogation, but these tended to yield information about the German front lines only. And the Germans were defending in great depth. For Rommel and others recognized the vital role of the Bourguébus ridge in preventing access to the Falaise corridor. Whether the Allied blow came from the west (past Hill 112), directly through Caen, or via the east of Caen was almost immaterial. The ridge was a backstop.

Allied intelligence failed to identify the front line correctly. On the German right, south of Caen, stood the 346. Division, a static coastal defence infantry unit which had nevertheless performed creditably since D-Day. To the German left, the newly arrived and quite fresh 272. Division, had replaced 1. SS-*Panzerdivision, Leibstandarte,* in the line.

In the centre was the infantry of 16. *Luftwaffenfelddivision*, battered, ill-supplied, and ill-trained. In the words of a 21. *Panzerdivision* officer,

> *This air force division was built up and formed from workshop companies, clerks, and cooks who changed their spoons against* [for] *rifles, and therefore were not very familiar with this* [infantry] *mission. They had to protect us from surprise and British patrols.*[8]

More senior commanders had deplored this formation of independent *Luftwaffe* formations instead of absorbing the manpower into standard army units. Von Manstein wrote:

> *To form these excellent troops into divisions within the framework of the Luftwaffe was sheer lunacy. Where were they to get the necessary close-combat training? ...where were they to get the battle experience? ...where was the Luftwaffe to find divisional, regimental, and battalion commanders?*

But the divide-and-rule politics of Hitler's *Reich* preserved a separate identity for Goering's *Luftwaffe*. Accordingly, 16. *FD* were given the task best suited to their skills, placed in the front line as an *'Infanterieschleier'*, a thin infantry 'veil' to mask the defences. In other words, they were expendable.

So much for the front line. Behind the *Infanterieschleier* German dispositions were even less clear. As infantry units summoned to the new front were gradually completing their long journey to Normandy, the Allies' great concern was that *Panzer* divisions hitherto holding the line would be released into reserve, and so restore the German high command's ability to regain the strategic initiative. Already, 276. *Infanteriedivision* had relieved *Panzer Lehr*, whose subsequent emergence on the American front was cause for some consternation. Likewise on the Caen front, behind the veil of infantry, contact had actually been lost with three key units: 1. SS-*Panzerdivision* (the *Leibstandarte*), 12. SS *Panzerdivision* (the redoubtable *Hitlerjugend*) and the greater part of 21. *Panzerdivision*. Allied intelligence took comfort in reports that all three had taken a battering and were licking their wounds. But the extent of their suffering was exaggerated and, most crucially, it was not realized that all three remained in the area and capable of intervening in the GOODWOOD operation.

Behind the forward screen, a layered defence extended further back than the most pessimistic Allied assessments allowed. This German tactic of defence in depth, developed during the First World War and honed in three years of bitter fighting on the Russian front, proved effective in Normandy. The front lines were thinly manned to minimize losses to the expected opening artillery barrage. Behind this veil, German defensive lines were deep, absorbing the impact of assault by a numerically superior enemy, forward forces sacrificing themselves to slow the advance and buying time for reinforcements to arrive. As soon as the enemy was brought to a halt, German doctrine insisted on immediate counter-attack, before the attacking force could establish itself on the objective, before it could draw breath, reorganize, and re-provision.

First, where intelligence placed remnants of 125. *Panzergrenadierregiment*, there stood in fact the greater part of 21. *Panzerdivision*. The 125. *PzGrRgt.* did indeed hold the centre of the battlefield, but on their left in the eastern outskirts of Caen was its sister regiment, 192. *PzGrRgt.* And on its right, unusually

The 7.5 cm Pak 40: an effective tank killer.

far forward, was the bulk of the divisional tank force, 22. *Panzerregiment*. A third layer lay further back: the antitank, reconnaissance, and artillery regiments of 21. *Panzerdivision* held positions actually on and behind the Bourguébus ridge line, while further back still was a broad belt of anti-aircraft artillery, mostly equipped with the much-feared 8.8cm dual-purpose gun. Further back still, though close enough to be able to reinforce the coming battle, were the *Leibstandarte* and the *Hitlerjugend* divisions. But before these, squarely in the path of the attack, lay 21. *Panzerdivision*.

Feuchtinger

In 1944, the commander of the newly re-created 21. *Panzerdivision* was the forty-nine year old Egdar Feuchtinger. A professional artilleryman, Feuchtinger had served continuously since the First World War. With the rise to power of the Nazi regime, Feuchtinger's political and social skills were noted in high places, and from 1935 to 1937 he distinguished himself in the organization of the annual Nürnberg rally, the *Parteitag*, and so he became known personally to Hitler and Goebbels. These contacts did not spare him from service on the Russian front, where he commanded a regiment of artillery. But from March 1943, Feuchtinger was posted to serve in occupied France.

Generalmajor Egdar Feuchtinger

This service was agreeable to Feuchtinger, all the more so since under his command was the remarkable Alfred Becker, whose workshops at Maisons-Laffitte to the west of Paris gave Feuchtinger the opportunity to maintain a 'special headquarters' within easy reach of the fleshpots of the city to which he became a frequent visitor. With the creation of 21. *Panzerdivision* and his own elevation to *Generalmajor*, Feuchtinger felt empowered to conduct himself in a manner which many of his fellow officers saw as 'bohemian' and the management of his division was widely held to be overly *laissez-faire*. What was ultimately to count most severely against the general was his absence from his unit on the critical invasion night of 5-6 June. And his absence was criticised all the more when it became known that not only had he been in Paris, but was spending the night with his lady friend, a well known, black comédienne. However, for the time being at least, Feuchtinger's contacts and political allies enabled him to shrug off criticism.

Feuchtinger needed all the influence at his disposal to prepare his division for combat. The re-created 21. *Panzerdivision* inherited a glorious reputation from its predecessor, which had fought the length and breadth of North Africa before going 'into the bag' at the final capitulation in Tunisia. But it inherited little more. In terms of equipment, it was at first decreed that the division's *Panzerregiment* should be equipped with captured French armour. Only after much string pulling did Feuchtinger achieve the grudging supply of *Panzer* IVs for one of the two tank battalions. No less important, recognizing his own lack of military experience, Feuchtinger was able to use his influence to draft into 21. *Panzerdivision* some extremely capable officers.

Becker's Batteries

Major Alfred Becker

One of the most distinctive features of the 21. *Panzerdivision* in Normandy was its remarkable assortment of armoured vehicles. These and the man behind them were to exert an important influence over the unfolding battle.

Alfred Becker was a forty-four year old engineer from Krefeld. Although technical director of his uncle's textile machinery firm, the army was a continuing theme in Becker's life. Volunteering in 1914, he served as an artilleryman before his fifteenth birthday, and was to win the Iron Cross at both Verdun and Cambrai before succumbing to poison gas only weeks before the war's end. Becker continued to be a keen member of the Krefeld artillery reserve, and in September 1939 was again called to the colours.

Becker's long experience as an artilleryman convinced him that modern warfare demanded better mobility for the guns. In the Netherlands in 1940, Becker's horse-drawn 12. *Batterie* of 227. *Artillerieregiment* had been immobilized by poor roads; by the end of the campaign he had dispensed with horsepower, his entire battery towed by captured vehicles. This was only the start. Becker began to organize the collection of dozens of broken down French vehicles from the 1940 battlefields. He pulled strings to secure twenty tonnes of 20mm armour plate from Hannover, and began to mount artillery pieces on the armoured chassis. Becker's particular skill gained official notice, enough to have him withdrawn from a posting to the Eastern Front where his artillery had repelled massed Russian tank attacks around Leningrad. Now Becker was personally directed by Albert Speer, with Hitler's blessing, to embark on a more systematic conversion of derelict enemy tanks to fill gaps in the German order of battle.

First in Spandau, later at *Baustab*, Becker based in Paris, supervised the redesign and reconditioning of over 1,800 vehicles, half of these armoured fighting vehicles. An artilleryman himself, *Generalmajor* Feuchtinger was quick to harness the enterprise of Becker for his own 21. *Panzerdivision*, thereby gaining not only a valuable source of scarce equipment but also, as time was to tell, a most efficient combat leader. Now a major commanding *Sturmgeschütz Abteilung 200*, Becker led a force of 600 men, in five batteries. But this was no ordinary assault gun battalion. Becker's batteries were not truly *Sturmgeschütz*, nor did they function as such.

The role of the German assault gun units had originally been to provide the infantry with mobile fire support to overwhelm enemy strongpoints. This demanded heavily armoured vehicles capable of moving through enemy fire to deliver close support. As weapons and tactics evolved, so did the *Sturmgeschütz*, whose short, direct-fire gun designed for High Explosive rounds was increasingly replaced with longer, higher velocity 7.5cm guns capable of an effective antitank role; in some cases the short 7.5cm cannon was replaced by a larger 10.5cm howitzer.

Early in the war, the German armoured units learned that the most effective tank killer was often not another tank, but a dedicated antitank gun. Time and again in the desert campaign, German tank units would lead Allied tanks on to hidden 'screens' of antitank guns, which accounted for a high proportion of Allied tank losses. While 21. *Panzerdivision* had its own dedicated antitank battalion, two batteries armed with the formidable 8.8cm *Pak 43*, Becker's batteries were also to be employed primarily in the tank-killing role. The vehicles were not constructed to be *Sturmgeschütz*. The guns under Becker at

French Hotchkiss H-39 chassis with a 7.5 cm Pak 40 gun.

GOODWOOD were mounted on Hotchkiss H-39 hulls, a twelve ton French light tank. Designed to carry a turret with a 3.7cm gun, these diminutive chassis were dwarfed by the long 7.5cm Pak 40 antitank guns or heavy 10.5 cm *leFH16* howitzers perched on them. And even though their armour plate was carefully designed to maximize the protection offered, there was a limit to the weight that the chassis could carry. Frontal armour of 40mm was that limit. The fact that these guns were open-topped took them further from the realm of the *Sturmgeschütz*. In the early days of the Normandy invasion, Becker's batteries proved woefully vulnerable in close action. Henceforth, far from wading into the thick of the battle, Becker's force would engage an advancing enemy from long range, and use their mobility to relocate before their vulnerability was put to the test.

As the importance of the antitank gun as a tank killer became understood, so did its weaknesses. In the early desert campaigns, the lack of a long range High Explosive round often prevented Allied tanks from engaging enemy antitank guns with their main armament, and attempting to close to machine gun range all too often proved fatal. By 1944, most Allied tanks had dual-purpose main guns, capable of firing both Armour Piercing rounds against armour and High Explosive rounds against 'soft' targets. In such an environment, the antitank gun had two potential defences. The first was concealment. The towed antitank gun could be 'dug in' and camouflaged, a process taking up to a day, with covered approaches allowing the crew to come and go unseen. Gunners would fire from concealment. They remained dependent on nearby infantry to keep the enemy at arm's length, though generally the gunners were unwilling to allow supporting infantry too close lest by 'milling around' the emplacement they might give away its location. A British artillery major in Normandy commented:

> antitank gunnery had always placed great responsibility on the Number Ones, now however they were having to deal not just with the occasional enemy tank but also having to contend with infiltration into the gun positions by enemy infantry.[9]

The price of concealment was loss of mobility. Frequently in Normandy, units being relieved would leave their antitank guns in place to be taken over by the relieving unit, rather than risk revealing the concealed position.

So, the second defence employed by antitank units was mobility. In the open desert, the British had frequently opted to sacrifice all pretence of concealment and leave the antitank guns mounted (*en portée*) on their prime movers. Firing from the back of a lorry without any protection, the guns at least could attempt to drive rapidly away when trouble threatened. By 1944, these *impromptu* arrangements were replaced by Allied antitank guns mounted in open-topped turrets on fully-tracked chassis. In theory, the two forms of antitank gun were complementary. When enemy ground was captured, self-propelled guns would move in to defend against armoured counter-attack until such time as the towed guns were emplaced, whereupon the SP guns would pull out and leave infantry and the barely-visible guns to hold the ground.

In practice, the Normandy battleground proved difficult for towed antitank guns, and especially so for the attacking side. Captain Wolley of 65/Antitank Regiment recorded the difficulty of manoeuvring the unwieldy 17-pounder antitank guns:

> The towed guns, known as 'pheasants' because of their long barrels and trails, were very difficult to tow, to man-handle and to conceal. It was difficult to find an adequate towing vehicle, even the [American] White half-track scout cars found the guns too heavy with the result that the vehicle clutches would soon wear out. In the narrow roads and lanes of the bocage country, the guns became an embarrassment and were not easy to get off the roads. With an advancing army we were constantly

deploying, then moving on to the next position, and saw very little action against tanks.

In fact, in mid-July an underutilized troop of Crusader antiaircraft tanks was attached to the regiment in order to help the overtaxed half-tracks to tow the big 17-pounders.[10]

In theory, the five batteries of *Sturmgeschütz Abteilung* 200 each had ten guns mounted on Hotchkiss tracked chassis: six of these ten carrying long 7.5cm *Pak* 40 antitank guns; the remaining four dwarfed by 10.5cm leFH18/40 howitzers. In practice, the equipment varied from time to time. Becker's engineers struggled to keep non-standard vehicles in fighting order. At one point in June, the unit's strength report lists only four batteries operational, with a total of seventeen (not thirty!) *Pak*-40 and twenty four rather than twenty howitzers, some of those the leFH16 model, relics of the First World War. The precise numbers on 18 July may never be known, but it seems certain that five batteries were operational at the start of the battle. And whatever the number of guns, the high state of training and efficiency was a constant, reflected in the unit's effective performance on the day.

According to the tactical plan, the antitank guns would seek hidden firing positions overlooking the likely enemy advance while the howitzers, capable of indirect fire, would be sited 500 to 1,000 metres to the rear. Overseeing each battery was an armoured command vehicle, from which the whole unit would be orchestrated by means of Becker's special ultra-low frequency radios (operating on frequencies not monitored by Allied radio interception). Typically, the forward antitank guns would sit-out the customary opening bombardment, then when enemy armour came within killing range of a kilometre or less, all six would commence accurate rapid fire. The 7.5cm gun's optics combined with the high profile of the Sherman tank frequently enabled first-shot hits to be achieved, and having secured one hit anywhere on a Sherman, a second was rarely necessary. Should the enemy advance uncomfortably close to the first line (that is, within a few hundred metres), the vehicles would pull back to pre-arranged positions, covered by indirect-fire smoke and High Explosive from the rearward howitzers, which would themselves leap-frog back behind the new positions.

At dawn of 18 July, the five batteries were established in a checkerboard formation, with overlapping fields of fire, in the villages of Démouville (*1.Bttr.*), Giberville (*2.Bttr.*), Grentheville (*3.Bttr.*), and the farms of le Mesnil-Frémentel (*4.Bttr.*) and le Prieuré (*5.Bttr.*). As a defence against enemy infantry, each battery was supported by a reduced-strength company of about twenty-five *Panzergrenadiere.*

Von Luck's *Panzer* Grenadiers

By 1944, Hans von Luck had a distinguished combat record in the Poland and France campaigns, and with the *Afrika Korps* in the desert. Now earmarked for command of the *Panzer* regiment of the *élite Panzer Lehr* Division, his transfer was intercepted by the well-connected Feuchtinger. Spotting a promising young officer with extensive experience, Feuchtinger had no hesitation in giving von Luck command of one of his division's two *Panzergrenadier* regiments.

Hans von Luck.

In 125. *Panzergrenadierregiment*, von Luck found a mixture of experienced but tired veterans of the Russian front, and a larger number of young replacements fresh from home. He also found a variety of equipment. In theory, his first battalion should have been entirely equipped with armoured personnel vehicles, his second with unarmoured motor transport. In practice, much of the transport was lacking, and much of what he had was extemporized from captured vehicles. The men were tired. Among the first to engage the enemy on 6 June, they had undergone a month of bitter fighting. Still, the men and the equipment were substantially superior to those of the thin screen of *Luftwaffe* troops, and although they were overdue for a period of rest, *General der Panzertruppen* Eberbach personally ordered that they remain in defensive positions behind the forward screen.

So it came about that – far from being pulled out of the line – elements of the 21. *Panzerdivision* were at the core of the defence south of Caen. In early July, von Luck's energy and experience were recognized by Feuchtinger who gave him increasing responsibility. His command of the two infantry battalions of 125. *Panzergrenadierregiment* was broadened into a *Kampfgruppe* including artillery assets, the *Luftwaffe* infantry battalion in the

Oberst Hermann von Oppeln-Bronikowski.

screen immediately ahead, and effective command over Major Becker's batteries, with whom the *Panzergrenadiere* were already well integrated. To this day, the German term '*Kampfgruppe*' means rather more than simply a 'battle group'; it conveys an *ad hoc* formation with a common understanding of tactics under dynamic leadership. Von Rosen's was an integrated command capable of defence in considerable depth.

Von Oppeln-Bronikovski's *Panzers*

As mentioned above, the armoured regiment of 21. *Panzerdivision* was initially denied German tanks, and had to make do with reconditioned versions of 1940-vintage French tanks. By the summer of 1944, *Panzerregiment 22* had acquired not only a distinguished leader, *Oberst* Hermann von Oppeln-Bronikowski, but also its first battalion received a complement of long-barrelled *Panzer* IV. These were involved in some of the

A Panzer IV of 22 *Panzerregiment* at the Lirose railway crossing (see page 107).

earliest armoured counter-attacks of D-Day. When finally released from reserve (on the personal order of LXXXIV *Korps* commander *General der Artillerie* Marcks who fumed with indignation at Feuchtinger's late arrival and failure to act), they penetrated north of Caen almost to the sea at Lion-sur-Mer. Sixteen of their tanks were lost on that day, and in the weeks that followed losses continued to mount in desperate defensive actions on the plateau north of Caen.

By 18 July, the fifty surviving *Panzer* IV were in forward positions. For a *Panzer* leader as experienced as Oppeln-Bronikowski, this was as unwelcome as it was unconventional. German doctrine favoured using the mobility of armour to counter-attack from reserve rather than defending forward positions. Feuchtinger would have allowed the experienced officer free rein, but *Generalfeldmarschall* Erwin Rommel had other ideas.

Convinced of the need for forward defences to prevent an Allied lodgement, Rommel had been thwarted on 6 June by orders that armour reserves could only be released on the order of the *Führer*. That morning, while Hitler slept and none in the *Führerhauptquartier* saw fit to wake him, much of the armoured strike force was held back, awaiting orders. Visiting Feuchtinger on the afternoon of 15 July, Rommel expressed his displeasure at the inactivity of 21. *Panzerdivision* on 6 June. He criticised especially the placement of its tanks so far behind the coast. *Generalmajor* Feuchtinger was not to be cowed. He pointed out to his superior that Rommel had ample opportunity to correct the placement of the tanks when he visited on two occasions just before the invasion: on 11 May and 18 May. The debate grew warmer. Rommel hotly accused Feuchtinger of absence from his unit on the night of the invasion. Feuchtinger countered, reminding his superior of the important elements of his division 'loaned out' to other units at the time of the invasion and pointed out – not without reason though perhaps without tact – that Rommel too had been away on leave at that crucial time. Still, Rommel remained the superior authority and had his way. 21. *Panzerdivision* was ordered to site its remaining tanks to the fore: ten *Panzer* IV covering the western sector Colombelles – Cuverville; the remainder (the number unconfirmed, probably around forty) on the eastern flank between Banneville and Emiéville.

Von Rosen's Tigers

The 503. *schwere Panzer-Abteilung* was a heavy tank unit which had served in Russia. Its Tiger tanks had performed with distinction both in a 'fire brigade' role, and as the spearhead in major offensives, including Operation ZITADELLE, the cataclysmic tank battle of Kursk. The battalion was withdrawn to re-equip in Germany but its relief was short-lived, as the Normandy invasion signalled its imminent move to France.

All armies face the dilemma of whether to gather their best soldiers into *corps d'élite*, or to spread them widely to increase the overall standard. By command of the Nazi regime, great development and production resources were devoted to the manufacture of relatively small numbers of Tiger tanks, and Hitler's original inclination was to give each *Panzerdivision* its own Tiger spearhead. But the role of a Tiger battalion was so specialized that in the end these immensely valuable weapons were organized in battalions separate from the *Panzer* divisions.

An independent Tiger battalion had about a thousand men and up to fifty Tiger tanks. In combat, the Tiger dominated its battlefield. The *Tigerfibel* (instruction manual) bluntly stated, 'It can stand up to anything.' For much of the war, this was incontestable. One commander, Alfred Rubbel, recalls,

> *The Tiger had won the race between armor protection and armor-piercing rounds. Not much could get at the Tiger man.*[11]

Consequently the Tiger men became supremely self-confident, coming to regard themselves as an *élite*, the *créme-de-la-créme* of the *Panzertruppen*. This self-image was only reinforced as they proved their worth in combat, and senior commanders called out for the support of Tiger battalions. Such was the crews' impression of impregnability that discipline and combat doctrine were often set aside; instead of seeking concealment, Tiger commanders arrogantly flaunted their tanks before the enemy. In Russia this worked. When the Tiger appeared in the defensive line, Russians attacks would often falter; conversely, the German infantry divisions, thinly stretched and bled white on the Russian steppe, took heart from their appearance (though on occasion Tiger tanks withdrawing for routine refuelling and resupply might trigger a wholesale abandonment of infantry positions).

Only three Tiger battalions fought in Normandy. Two were SS-*Abteilungen* (101. and 102.), each assigned to an SS-*Panzer*

Korps. The 503. was a *Wehrmacht* unit (various accounts have said it was SS; these are mistaken as the unit contained no SS personnel) and was directed to support the LXXXVI. *Armeekorps* in the Caen sector. Before leaving Germany, the unit received new tanks and, unexpectedly early, on 16 June, 1. *Kompanie* received its first examples of the new Mark Two Tiger, the *Königstiger*. In many respects this new 'King' Tiger was a considerable improvement on its predecessor, with heavier armour, a heavier gun, and a much faster turret traverse. However, for all their cost, these technical improvements were largely wasted in the Normandy fighting. The original Tiger already had armour sufficient to face the antitank guns it was to encounter in the west, and a gun whose accuracy and weight already represented considerable 'overkill' against any armour it might meet outside Russia. In the event, the first action of the 503. *Abteilung* in Normandy was to showcase the strengths of the earlier Tiger I.

In the small hours of 11 July, 153 Brigade (of 51st Highland Division) launched a major raid southwards down the east bank of the Orne River. Their objective was to seize the huge metal works of Colombelles long enough for Royal Engineers to demolish the twin chimneys which afforded German observers a clear view over the entire sector. Though supported by heavy artillery and tanks of 148/Royal Armoured Corps, the night attack progressed slowly. Woken at 05.00 hours, the young *Leutnant* von Rosen commanding 3. *Kompanie* (whose commander was deputizing for the battalion *Hauptmann*) was informed that the forward defences were shattered, and ordered to prevent a breakthrough. Halting his column of thirteen Tigers

'Not much could get at the Tiger man.'

just short of Giberville, von Rosen reconnoitred forward on a motor cycle. Viewing the battlefield from an upstairs window, an observation post of Becker's 2. *Batterie*, he watched Sherman tanks manoeuvring towards Colombelles, two kilometres away. He returned to lead his company into action. Taking his time, von Rosen planed his attack with care, forming the thirteen Tiger tanks into three sections, with a small reserve. Only then did they move into the open. Completely unconcealed, they were quickly spotted and a violent torrent of fire descended, which the heavy tanks shrugged off.

A brief halt, and von Rosen gave the order to advance in successive bounds. No one moved. Realizing at last that his radio aerial had been shot away, von Rosen led by example, followed by the central section of tanks. The other sections conformed in the standard assault pattern: one section at a time moving in 500 metre bounds while the other two gave covering fire. Closing to 200 metres of the 148/RAC Shermans, the Tiger tanks were deluged with hits, but no serious damage was done, while Sherman after Sherman exploded into flame. Within thirty minutes of the start of the action, a dozen British tanks were burning and two officers' mounts that ran into each other trying to escape were captured intact. The British raid was broken, at great loss, and after several hours of manoeuvring around the plain dodging the retribution of the Royal Artillery (directed by spotting aircraft), the thirteen Tigers left the field, with their captured Shermans, and with a re-formed German defensive line in place.

The Artillery

Much has been made in accounts of GOODWOOD of the strength of the German artillery deployed in depth on and behind the Bourguébus ridge, out of range of British artillery and largely untouched by aerial bombardment. A much-quoted British source records:

> 78 'eighty-eights' and 12 other heavy flak guns... 194 field pieces and 272 'nebelwerfer' (six-barrelled mortars)... From these 1,632 barrels they could drench the whole area between the Orne and the Dives.[12]

This impressive total, apparently concocted by Rommel himself, has influenced many later writers, Germans included. Most of the '194 field pieces' were supporting the forward units, including the artillery organic to the 16. *Luftwaffe* and the 21. *Panzer* divisions. A variety of types and calibres, including large numbers of captured Russian tubes, they were typically directed by forward observers accompanying the forward infantry. As for the *Nebelwerfer*, most were deployed well to the north of the Bourguébus ridge.

These highly specialized weapons require some explanation. They had some undoubted strengths: they could deliver very large quantities of 150mm rocket-propelled High Explosive rounds in a matter of seconds, preceded by the monstrous howling that led to their being known as 'Moaning Minnies' or (by the Americans) 'Screaming Meemies'. Along with conventional mortars, they accounted for a high percentage of Allied infantry casualties in Normandy. But they were relatively short-ranged, and their inaccuracy reduced their effectiveness. To achieve the same effect as conventional artillery against a point target, the *Nebelwerfer* required greater quantities of ammunition, and the *Nebelwerfer* batteries were short of ammunition on 18 July. Even the morale effect of the screaming 'incoming' bombs wore off as troops became accustomed to them and realised that sound entrenchments (ideally with overhead cover) were a good defence. The most effective use of *Nebelwerfer* was against a newly taken position, previously registered by the German artillery, before the assaulting Allied infantry could properly dig in. Many a time, advancing infantry would find the welcome shelter of a hedgerow-lined orchard deceptive as a barrage of bombs burst in the treetops, raining shards of metal and turning the refuge into a slaughterhouse. The *Nebelwerfer* themselves relied on concealment. While the crews could fire the rockets by remote control, the weapons' backblast precluded their firing from fortified bunkers. Commonly sited just inside treelines, they gave away their positions with darts of flame and clouds of smoke; once spotted by the enemy, reloading or relocation became hazardous. The flimsy firing apparatus was especially vulnerable to area bombardments and though the numbers lost in the GOODWOOD preparatory bombardment may never be known, they were certainly high.

The '78 eighty-eights' have attracted particular attention, largely due to the mythic status of the weapon amongst Allied troops. Most of the claimed '78 eighty-eights' and the twelve

The incomparable Pak 43.

heavy (possibly 10.5cm) antiaircraft guns belonged to *Generalkommando* III. *Flakkorps*, and it is important to note that few of these (save a single battery of four 8.8cm *Flak* sent forward to Cagny) were to play a part in the forthcoming land battle. The three *Flaksturmregimenter* that comprised the corps were distributed far to the south and east of Bourguébus. Not only was the *Flakkorps* commander, *Generalleutnant* Wolfgang Pickert, independent of Feuchtinger's 21. *Panzerdivision*, but he had strict instructions from *Panzergruppenkommando-West* (HQ *Panzer* Group West) that his role was to protect the Caen-Falaise road from air attack. His batteries were accordingly sited in a wide arc from Thury-Harcourt to Troarn. In a sketch of his dispositions, Pickert confirms that at the dawn of 19 July most of his antiaircraft guns still remained well clear of the land battle.

This was by no means unusual. Contrary to popular belief, in the Normandy campaign the *Flak* 18/36, the '88' so dreaded by the tank men, was primarily employed in the antiaircraft role. True, even in the hands of the *Luftwaffe* the 8.8cm antiaircraft gun was equipped to fire antitank rounds. But its disadvantages in an antitank role were many. The piece was big, hard to entrench and camouflage. It was unwieldy, requiring time to 'limber up' for transportation. The gun *could* be fired while limbered, but only with difficulty, in a narrow frontal arc, unless risking a sideways shot whose recoil was likely to damage the carriage and possibly immobilize the piece in the face of the enemy. Most important of all, Allied air supremacy over Normandy put air defence at a premium. The 88 crews' first priority – and the main focus of the *Luftwaffe* crews' training – remained the antiaircraft role, in which they were most effective. As an expedient the *Flakkorps* gunners were prepared to deliver indirect (High Explosive) fire in support of the front line units, but only as a last resort would they normally expect to engage the enemy with direct fire. In fact, the 7.5cm round of the standard German antitank gun of the day, the *Pak 40*, was only marginally less likely to destroy the Sherman and Cromwell tanks encountered at GOODWOOD, and its light weight and low profile made it overall more effective in a front line antitank role. A Sherman tank crew was unlikely to know whether their tank was brewed by an 88 or a well camouflaged *Pak 40* firing with little muzzle flash and less smoke, and on later inspection of the wreck the holes would appear very much the same size. The figures tell the story: in the course of the Normandy campaign, Pickert's *Flakkorps* accounted for 462 aircraft vs. 92 tanks, of which 12 were attributed to hand-held *Panzerfäuste*.

The guns occupying the Bourguébus ridge on the morning of 18 July, emplaced above and behind Bourguébus and Hubert-Folie, belonged to the Army. The indirect-fire artillery pieces on the reverse slopes of the ridge were screened by the specialist antiaircraft and antitank battalions of 21. *Panzerdivision*, and they in turn were protected by the men of their divisional reconnaissance and pioneer battalions. After the war, von Luck criticized this siting of the divisional heavy antiaircraft and antitank units so far to the rear of the battle, citing the reluctance of Feuchtinger, the former artillery officer, to expose his artillery to risk. The criticism appears unfair. These guns were indeed sited out of range of the British artillery, but in positions offering incomparable fields of vision to match their long range. They included a relatively small number of tubes: seventeen dedicated antitank guns, the incomparable *Pak 43*, belonging to *Panzerjäger-Abteilung* 200; and a further eight heavy antiaircraft guns, *Flak 36* of the division's *Flak-Abteilung* 305.[13] Few in

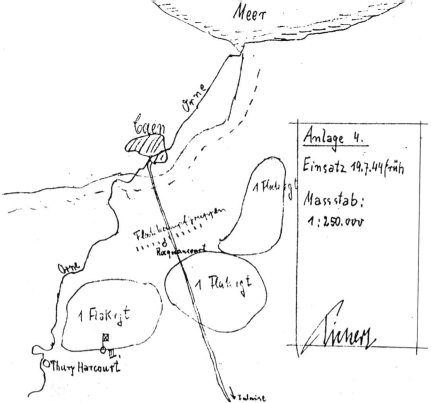

Wolfgang Pickert's own signed sketch of his regiment's deployment on the morning of 19 July. Few of his '88s' engaged tanks during the battle.

number, far from the hundreds of guns of some accounts of the battle, but capable nevertheless of immense execution from commanding heights ideally suited to the range and potency of these heavy guns.

References

1. Blumenson, p 187.
2. *From Normandy to the Ruhr,* H G Guderian, 2001, ISBN 0-9666389-7-2, p 45.
3. Ashley Hart, p 118.
4. Militärgeschichtliches Forshungsamt Dokumentärantrag B287.
5. *Ultra in the West,* Ralph Bennett, 1979, ISBN 0 09 139330 2, p 103.
6. NorthAG Battlefield Tour 1988 (TDRC 08909).
7. Blumenson p 181.
8. Von Luck interview at Staff College, Camberley, 1979.
9. Major Oakes, in Bastin, p 229.
10. Bastin, p 229.
11. *The Combat History of Schwere Panzer-Abteilung 503,* 2000, ISBN 0-921991-55-X, p 19.
12. Wilmot, p 396 (his source for the figures quoted was Manfred Rommel, from his father's papers, the purpose for which the numbers were prepared is unknown but they appear optimistic).
13. Note: the total of twenty-five guns is the best estimate of the number operational on 18 July, based on the last strength return before the battle: *Meldung* dated 1 July, 1944.

CHAPTER SEVEN

MONDAY 17 JULY: THE EVE OF BATTLE

The Stealthy Appoach

The British plan to transfer three armoured divisions around the north side of Caen to positions from which they could cross the Caen Canal and Orne River, turn right, and funnel through unmarked minefields was breathtaking in its audacity. To attempt to execute this in total secrecy would seem ludicrous. But this was the serious intent. Movements were at night, vehicles and troops lying low by day. On Sunday, 16 July, there was a brief panic in VIII Corps Headquarters when news came in that a photo-reconnaissance Spitfire had been shot down as it photographed the proposed GOODWOOD battlefield. Corps artillery was brought down on the crash site and fighter-bombers scrambled to obliterate any evidence of the intended offensive.[1]

In hindsight, the British obsession with secrecy was quite pointless. 'Sepp' Dietrich knew full well that an attack would eventually be launched towards the Bourguébus ridge. Whether it came from the west, over Hill 112, or from the east, around Caen, mattered little. Indeed, the fall of Caen simplified his deployments, allowing him to 'concentrate on essentials'. Dietrich had a simple philosophy, and believed that when the time came he would be able to hear the enemy coming by the trick (learned in Russia) of putting his ear to the ground. (The residents of Caen later confirmed that the movement of the armoured divisions did indeed resonate through the chalky strata and was heard clearly in their underground shelters.) Since the failure of

'Sepp' Dietrich

The expendable infantry patrol the approaches to the metalworks.

the 11 July attempt to demolish the tall chimneys of the Caen metalworks, lookouts in these lofty posts with a view to the sea and beyond could hardly fail to miss the activity below, as new roads were bulldozed and Bailey Bridges thrown across river and canal. On the night of 16-17 July, *Luftwaffe* aircraft took flare light photographs of the new Orne bridges, revealing the one-way flow of traffic.[2] All units in the Caen sector were duly alerted and Rommel's headquarters forecast a *'large-scale attack which is expected from the evening of the seventeenth for making a breakthrough across the Orne.'* On 17 July, Rommel made it a priority to view the defences in this sector.

The Demise of the Fox

On the afternoon of 17 July, *Generalfeldmarschall* Erwin Rommel had much to occupy his mind. His precise thoughts as his Horch staff car sped eastward along Normandy roads have been the subject of long debate and may never be precisely resolved. But it is safe to say that his over-riding concern was the lack of any realistic prospect of German victory. Rommel's reputation as a 'Desert Fox' had been forged in the fluid desert campaigns of the *Afrika Korps*. There he had suffered from lack of equipment and supplies but so long as his triumphs lasted he had been granted a great degree of freedom to fight in his own style. His personal strengths of leadership and tactical creativity had been given free rein. Now in Normandy, for all his fame, inflated by Goebbels' propaganda machine, Rommel found his freedom of action narrowly constrained. He despaired of victory. In his last personal meeting with Hitler on 28 June, he had tried to 'speak bluntly' about the hopelessness of the military situation and even dared to raise the wider 'question of Germany'. But he had been summarily ordered to leave the room: 'I think it would be better like that'. Hitler remained unbending in the face of reason. On 1 July, Gehr von Schweppenburg was sacked for speaking his mind (to be replaced by Eberbach) and on the morning of 2 July Rundstedt 'resigned' (to be replaced as *Oberbefehlshaber* West by von Kluge). After just ten days in the job, von Kluge was already reporting the situation as 'grim'.

von Kluge

All key decisions relating to the defence of Normandy were subject to Hitler's approval. At first, Rommel's unconventional plan for the defence of Normandy had been approved. Contrary to normal German thinking, Rommel proposed to put all his force in the front line to prevent a landing, defending with very little depth and with the *Panzer* reserves close to the front. He maintained:

> *It is more important to have one Panzerdivision in the assaulted sector on D-Day than to have three there by D-plus-3. The first twenty four hours will be decisive.*

But even this plan was undone by Hitler, who demanded that the armoured reserves be held back for release only on his own authority. By mid-July, Rommel's freedom of movement was constrained alike by *Diktat* of the *Führer* and by the dominance of Allied air power. Ironically, and unbeknown to the Field Marshall, the Allied powers still saw Rommel as a sufficient threat to warrant an assassination attempt. Operation GAFF involved six men (and four pigeons, 'not to be regarded as extra rations'), dropped with orders to kill Rommel at la Roche Guyon.[3]

On 17 July Rommel had held meetings close to the front with

'Sepp' Dietrich of *I. SS-Panzer Korps* and Wilhelm Bittrich of *II. SS-Panzer Korps*. It may be that Rommel's final meeting with his corps commanders included discussion of the possibility of disobeying Hitler, whether by outright negotiation with the Western Allies or the gamble of unauthorized withdrawal from France to the Siegfried Line preparatory to a military coup within Germany. The truth is buried deep. After the failed assassination attempt of 20 July, German generals were wise to protest their loyalty to Hitler; after the war's end, many protested instead their disloyalty to the Hitler regime.

What is certain is that the corps commanders' assessments of the military situation focused on their concern over lack of air support.

We are not afraid of the enemy ground forces, 'Sepp' Dietrich maintained, *but we are helpless against the massed action by the air force.*

The concern of the *SS-Obergruppenführer* extended to his boss: Dietrich's parting advice was that as Rommel was travelling in daylight he should consider using a common *Kübelwagen* runabout in place of his distinctive *Horch* staff car. Ironically, this was the very advice that Rommel himself had offered to von Kluge on his arrival in Normandy: Kluge had at first dismissed the precaution, but soon swallowed his pride when he realised the true extent of Allied domination of the Normandy skies.

Rommel left his meetings early, at 16.00 hours, in order to return in good time from the *I. SS-Panzer Korps* headquarters at Urville (on the Falaise road south of Caen) to Army Group B headquarters at la Roche Guyon, on the River Seine. Normally the 200 kilometre journey could be accomplished in two hours; but in 1944 Rommel's driver Daniel had to contend with the threat from the air. The car wove its way past smoking wrecks on the main road, occasionally darting down less conspicuous side roads to make progress across country. The centre of Livarot was avoided as British fighter-bombers circled over the town, waiting for targets of opportunity. Then around 18.00 hours the *Horch* emerged from a side road onto the main N 175. The decision was made to sprint south along the highway to Vimoutiers, opting for speed at the cost of creating a conspicuous plume of dust. *Feldwebel* Holke on aircraft watch reported two aircraft peeling off in preparation for an attack. The driver accelerated in a vain effort to reach a side road a few

Rommel travelled in his distinctive *Horch* staff car alongside his driver *Gefreiter* Daniel.

hundred yards ahead which promised some cover. But the Spitfire won the race. Cannon shells ripped up the road surface and tore through the left side of the *Horch*. Wounded in his left arm and shoulder, Daniel lost control of the heavy car which plunged onward until it ran off the road, into a tree, and turned over in a ditch.

Moments later the wreck of the car smouldered with only the dead and dying inside. Holke and *Hauptmann* Lang had jumped clear. Braving further aircraft, they ran back to Rommel where he lay in the road. The Field Marshal appeared to be dying. Blood poured from his mouth and left eye; his face was peppered with broken glass from the car window. Shell fragments had hit his temple and left cheekbone, rendering him unconscious with a triple skull fracture. Remarkably, Rommel survived until transport was found. He was treated at a pharmacy in Livarot before being admitted to the *Luftwaffe* hospital at Bernay. But he would never again command troops in the field.

Night Moves

Concentration for the battle began on the night of 16/17 July. At nightfall, 3rd Infantry Division's 9 Brigade crossed to the east side of the Orne, closely followed by 11th Armoured Division's Main Headquarters and 159 (motorized infantry) Brigade Group. 159 Brigade settled into its allotted concentration area to the north of le Bas de Ranville. Finally, 3rd Division's 8 Brigade crossed the Orne.

Back to the east of the Orne River, 11th Armoured Division's 29 Brigade suffered the first of two night marches. Columns of vehicles struggled around the torn countryside and rubbled outskirts of Caen along narrow roads. Moving under cover of the brief summer night meant that drivers' eyes had to strain to follow the vehicle in front without colliding or straying onto verges or into surrounding fields which had yet to be cleared of thousands of mines. The strain became steadily greater as the warm night filled with dust and fumes. During the night of 17/18 July, 11th Armoured Division's armour made the river crossing: the three Sherman tank regiments of 29 Brigade followed by the Cromwell tanks of 2/Northamptonshire Yeomanry, due to support 159 Brigade in the battle to come. Finally arriving in the assembly area west of the river, it seemed to Bill Close:

> ...that 3/RTR reached its concentration area as much by luck as judgement and camouflaged ourselves among wrecked and burned-out gliders which had brought the 6th Airborne Division in on D-Day. We were told to stay out of sight and get as much rest as possible.[4]

Back on the west side of the Orne river both Guards Armoured and 7th Armoured Division formed up ready for the morning, the heads of both columns of vehicles 5,000 yards back from the

Each of the three crossing points had bridges for both tracks and wheeled vehicles.

bridges, while the Canadian 8 Brigade took its turn to cross (9 Brigade remaining on the west bank between Blainville and Bènouville).

Alongside the tank regiments of 11th Armoured Division came the attached motor infantry of 8/Rifle Brigade. David Stileman commanded 11 Platoon, G Company.

> It was about 1.00am that we arrived in this sea of golden corn strewn with gliders from the D Day landings. And the corn was so high that not only did it cover a Bren Gun Carrier but the whole area was so congested that one had to ask the driver to move up a few feet in order to open the door of ones vehicle. Along with our friends of A Squadron [3/Royal Tank Regiment] we had only two hours breather before making our way through the minefield.[5]

As usual, it was the officers who were last to grab a few hours of sleep. At 01.00 hours on 18 July, Stileman's G Company

commander Noel Bell was still on his feet, joining A Squadron commander Bill Close to view the entrances to the newly-cleared gaps in the minefields to the south. Both were impressed by the ordered scene: smart Military Police, entry lanes and minefields clearly marked with white tape as requested by 'Pip' Roberts. (In fact, in the fields to the south, work on the final mine clearances was still continuing under cover of darkness and would not be completed until 05.15 hours.) The two returned to supervise the lining up of vehicles, nose to tail in the attack formation. As the two were inspecting the start lines, VIII Corps headquarters received confirmation (about 01.45 hours) that the weather would permit flying without which the operation could not proceed. Operation GOODWOOD would take place that day: Wednesday, 18 July, with H-Hour confirmed as 07.45. The news was quickly passed down to all units. Officers took what sleep they could in the time remaining.

References

1. Jackson, p 92.
2. Wilmot, p 396.
3. *The SAS at War*, Anthony Kemp, 1971, ISBN 0-7195-4890-X.
4. Close, interview at Staff College, Camberley, 1979.
5. Stileman, interview at Staff College, Camberley, 1979.

CHAPTER EIGHT

THE AERIAL BOMBARDMENT

Tactical Airpower

Even with virtually complete command of the daytime skies over the Normandy battlefield, co-ordination of aircraft with the troops on the ground remained problematic throughout the campaign. Most forward Allied troops eventually had the experience of being attacked by their own aircraft, especially when advancing close to the enemy. Army doctrine was unprepared for the idea of close air support in such country, and even identification panels were at first rejected. Only on the eve of GOODWOOD were all tanks ordered to paint white panels on their turrets. This caused some consternation to the M10-equipped 144 Battery of 91/Antitank Regiment:

> We now have to paint the whole surface of the turret tops white for recognition by aircraft. This provided a problem for us as the M10s and my Crusader are lidless. There is a counterweight on the M10s so we put it there. As to my Crusader, we have painted a square 3 ft by 3 ft on the engine hatches at the back, disregarding a suggestion from Peter Maxwell that it ought to be painted on the Battery Commander's Balmoral. [The 91st were Argylls, and the Balmoral was their headdress.]

Expedients such as accompanying forward troops with Air Support Signals Units (ASSUs), experienced fighter pilots in radio contact with the supporting aircraft, proved hard to perfect. For GOODWOOD, a single Forward Control Post accompanied 'Pip' Roberts' division: a turretless Marmon Herrington armoured car which was knocked out on 18 July, leaving 11th Armoured unable directly to contact the fighter-bombers overhead. Thereafter, requests would have to go up through VIII Corps to the RAF, the rough position of targets to be marked with pink smoke.

The German troops quickly learned that survival depended on the care with which they camouflaged themselves and their weapons from aerial view. Moreover, prior to the start of the Normandy campaign, it had been recognized that active air defence would be a priority. Consequently, losses of fighters over the battlefield were high. Even during the campaign, Operational Research showed that fighter-bomber aircraft were remarkably ineffective at hitting tanks, with tank kills tending to be vastly overestimated. Trials against a captured Panther tank, immobile in the open, showed that a single air-launched rocket had barely a half-percent chance of hitting a tank: approximately four percent for a volley of eight rockets. Few German tanks were so exposed. One French civilian interviewed had witnessed a dozen air attacks on a single abandoned German half-track – no doubt each one recorded as a 'tank kill'. It now appears that around a hundred German AFVs were destroyed by aircraft in the Normandy campaign, against the loss of over 1,700 Allied ground attack aircraft. On the other hand, the number of German tanks abandoned by crews panicked by air attack was high – and the mere presence of Allied aircraft inhibited tactical manoeuvre. On 18 July, Canadian radio intercepted requests from *Leibstandarte* tanks to disengege from action on the Bourguébus ridge – requests denied due to Allied air activity.[2]

Seeds of Controversy
Through the early months of 1944, there was intense debate within the Allied command about how strategic air power would support the Normandy invasion. This was unsurprising. In the pre-war expansion of Britain's airpower, the Royal Air Force trebled in size in five years. Too much, it was felt, for one man to command, and so the force was split into three: Fighter Command, Bomber Command, and Coastal Command. So, remarkably, the Royal Air Force lacked a single commander. And within an air force conscious of its junior status alongside the navy and the army, Bomber Command continued the struggle to establish itself as a strategic force independent of the other Services. This was far from easy in the early years of war in the face of limited resources and (during the Battle of the Atlantic) effective subordination of the air arm to the needs of the Admiralty.

Up to the end of 1942, Allied bombardment of German military targets lacked any consistent strategy, and the arrival in Britain of American strategic air forces made consistency even harder to achieve. The experience of Bomber Command had

American B-17 Flying Fortresses engaged in day-light precision bombing.

been that day bombing proved too costly and so they preferred area bombing by night. The Americans arrived with their B17 'Flying Fortress', a purpose-built day bomber, equipped with the precision Norden bombsight and armed with enough machine guns to make a formation – in theory – self-defending. Ideally, the night bombers and the day bombers might have complemented each other. But Bomber Command and the US Air Force were still developing their ideas about the application of strategic air power, and were arriving at very different conclusions.

In January 1943 at Casablanca, Churchill strived to achieve a common strategy. A clear directive was decreed. A 'Combined Bomber Offensive' would aim to achieve:

> *...the progressive destruction and dislocation of the German military, industrial, and economic systems, and the undermining of the morale of the German people to the point where their capacity for armed resistance is fatally weakened.*[3]

Fine words, but the devil lay in the detail. Bomber Command's determined leader Air Chief Marshall Arthur Harris was committed to an unrelenting campaign against German cities. One night in 1940, at the height of the Blitz, watching the City of

London burning from the roof of the Air Ministry in King Charles Street, Harris famously commented to Portal, 'Well... they are sowing the wind.'[4] And now they would reap the whirlwind. Harris was determined to reduce Germany to an 'industrial desert', and to achieve this was prepared to deprive German workers of their sleep, their homes, and ultimately their lives. By contrast, the Americans' strategy was based on the paramount need to reduce Germany's air defences which threatened the day bombers, by striking at aircraft production and – crucially – at German fuel production.

With the planning of Operation OVERLORD, ideas about the direction of the strategic air forces became further divided. In November, 1943, the Allied Expeditionary Air Force, under Air Chief Marshall Sir Trafford Leigh-Mallory was created. This new force united the British 2nd Tactical Air Force, the American 9th Air Force, and the 'stay at home boys' of Air Defence Great Britain. Leigh-Mallory's force included no heavy bombers, though he realized that they would certainly be needed for the Normandy invasion. And Montgomery's staff were already assuming this support, including the heavy bombers in their military plans.

Harris welcomed the appointment in January, 1944, of Air Chief Marshall Sir Arthur Tedder, to be Eisenhower's direct deputy. But it soon became clear that Tedder had priorities very different from those of Harris and Spaatz. By early 1944, SHAEF's analysts were discounting both the *Luftwaffe* and the 'V' weapons as major threats to the invasion of Europe. A more productive goal target would be the interdiction (or blocking) of German logistics across France. An early plan for a concerted assault on key parts of the French rail network just prior to D Day was rejected: it was too dependent on good weather during the vital pre-invasion days. Professor Solly Zuckerman, scientific advisor to the Allied Expeditionary Air Force, analyzed the paralysis that had been caused to the rail network in Italy and proposed a similar, sustained campaign against the railways of France.

Harris and Spaatz were appalled. Burying their differences over strategic bombing, they united in opposition to the rail transport campaign. Churchill agreed. He favoured maintenance of strategic bombing; also he feared the impact on French opinion, voicing concern over a campaign that might 'kill 10,000 Frenchmen' and 'smear the good name of the Royal Air Force around the world'. As late as May, the Prime Minister was insisting that targets be chosen where fewer than a hundred Frenchmen risked being killed. Under pressure from Roosevelt, following Eisenhower's resignation threat (without all-out commitment to OVERLORD, he stated, he would 'simply have to go home'), Churchill conceded on 11 May.

The rail campaign was a success. Through April and May, 1,437 French locomotives were damaged by air attack (versus 292 by Resistance sabotage, which caused 20,000 uniformed German railway workers to be imported to supervise SNCF employees). 21 May heralded 'Chatanooga Day', after which fighter-bombers roamed freely, attacking all line targets. By 26 May, all the Seine rail crossings north of Paris were closed, and all remained closed through the next thirty days (bridge repairs were closely observed and when nearing completion the bridges were again broken). By June, traffic on the French railways was down to a third of the May level. As to Churchill's concern over the 10,000 French civilian casualties inflicted, Free French General Koenig was consulted and replied laconically, *'C'est la guerre'*. In March, 18,000 men of the Todt Organization had been redeployed from work on Hitler's 'Atlantic Wall' to

Units relied on rail transport.

keeping the railroads running; in May a further 10,000 were taken. Much later it was found that direct bombing of the Atlantic Wall fortifications had caused little physical damage; the diversion of the workforce was probably more effective. Moreover, the Germans were forced to increase their reliance on road transport, making their communications and logistics critically vulnerable to air attack in the weeks ahead.

Bombing the Battlefield

In the weeks following D Day, the air plan took an unexpected course. It had been predicted that once the troops were ashore in France the strategic bombers would revert to their accustomed role of pounding targets deep in the German heartlands. However, as early as the night of 14-15 June, Bomber Command was persuaded to send 337 heavy bombers against Aunay and Evrecy, road junctions important to the German build up south of the river Odon. Both places were flattened for no aircraft lost. Encouraged by this, Bomber Command again acceded to tactical intervention on 30 June, sending 266 Lancaster and Halifax heavy bombers on a low-level (4,000 feet) daylight strike against Villers-Bocage. Some of the last aircraft in the raid reported flying through clouds of red smoke: the brick dust of the small town. Villers-Bocage was pulverized and some slight delay imposed on the advancing 9. SS-*Panzerdivision*.

A week later, with Montgomery increasingly frustrated at the failure to take the D-Day objective of Caen, Operation

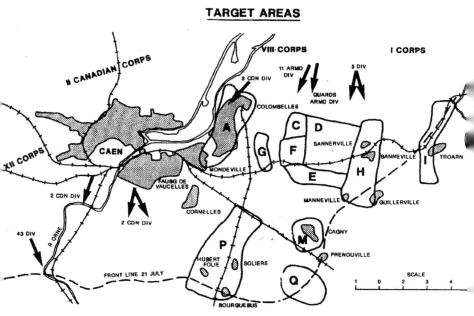

TARGET AREAS

CHARNWOOD was launched against the city's north-west outskirts. The 8 July assault was preceded on the evening of 7 July by a 467 bomber raid. Morale amongst the waiting attackers was raised by the impressive sight. Sadly for them, the bombardment came far too long before the first attack. Only later would the planners realise that the morale effect of heavy bombing was greater than its physical impact on well dug-in defenders, and that the effect wore off relatively rapidly. Moreover, in an attempt to limit 'friendly fire' casualties, the bomb line had been moved 6,000 yards beyond the Commonwealth forces' start lines; this took the bombing some distance behind the 12. SS-Panzerdivision 'Hitlerjugend' defenders. Most of the bombs' impact was felt by the civilian population (forbidden by the Germans to leave the city) and buildings of Caen itself. If anything, the bombardment discouraged the German defenders from falling back into the devastated city. When they finally retired, the rubble of Caen prevented a rapid Allied follow-up.

Harris objected to this use of his Bomber Command, '...diverting our best weapon from a military function... to one which it cannot effectively carry out'. Air Chief Marshal Sir Charles Portal feared,

We shall sooner or later reach a stage when almost the whole of the bomber effort has to be frittered away in small packets if the Army is to attack at all.

An embittered Tedder agreed, questioning the Army's competence to do their job, 'The army having been drugged with bombs, it is going to be a difficult process to cure the addicts.' Old enmities lingered.

Guns or Bombs

The GOODWOOD plan presented VIII Corps with a logistical nightmare. Three armoured divisions had to be pushed across the bottleneck of three improvised river crossings, then perform a right turn and advance four miles down a 1,500 yard corridor, barely wide enough to deploy a single armoured regiment. Most of the artillery that would normally be called upon to support a corps-level operation would be firing from the far, north-west side of Caen, and much of it would be near maximum range almost from the start. In theory, a 25-pounder field regiment located 3,000 yards behind the front line, with its effective range of 11,000 yards and a 90 degree arc of fire, should be able to dominate over thirty square miles of enemy territory. But batteries sited on the far (northern) side of Caen would be unable to influence large areas of the planned GOODWOOD battle. Moreover, for all the excellent qualities of the British 25-pounder field gun, its shell was relatively lightweight and against a well-entrenched enemy could only hope to keep heads down.[4] The problem was compounded by a shortage of artillery ammunition. This deficiency had to be made up by airpower. (By chance, for Bomber Command, a 'Goodwood' had long been code for a maximum-effort bombing raid.)

The Bombing

A Guards tank crewman recalled,

> *Possibly the only time in the history of the 2nd Battalion Grenadier Guards when all ranks were up before reveille was on 18 July 1944, for at 05.00 hours a distant thunder in the air brought all the sleepy-eyed tank crews out of their blankets. 1,000 Lancasters were flying in from the sea in groups of three or four at 3,000 feet. Ahead of them the pathfinders were scattering their flares and before long the first bombs were dropping.*

The sight was unusual. The night bombers so rarely seen in daylight flew low over the target, their black undersides ghostly above the morning mist. Flying just above the 3,000 foot reach of light antiaircraft fire, they began to release their deadly cargo in full view of the ground troops. For German observers, a nightmare began.

Werner Kortenhaus was with the tank regiment of *21. Panzerdivision*:

> *The men got into the tanks and closed the flaps, or crawled underneath for protection. We saw little dots detach themselves from the planes, so many of them that the crazy thought occurred to us: are those leaflets? We could hardly believe that they could all be bombs.*

Every one of the 'leaflets' was a 500 or a 1,000 pound bomb, delay-fused for cratering. For Kortenhaus, it was

> *...the most terrifying hours of our lives... Among the thunder of the explosions, we could hear the wounded scream and the insane howling of men who had been driven mad.*

There had previously been cases of *Panzer IV* tanks reduced to scrap by the chance impact of a large-calibre naval shell. But this was systematic destruction on an unparalleled scale. One by one, the *Panzer IV* of Kortenhaus' *Panzerregiment 22* were put out of action. Also in the area were the Tiger tanks of *503. s.Pz.Abt.* These were more sturdy, but succumbed nevertheless.

Only after July – after GOODWOOD – would objective studies of the effects of aerial bombardment of the battlefield yield the surprising result that it had been generally less effective than imagined. Two factors made the GOODWOOD bombing more effective than usual. Firstly, the German front line was held by inexperienced and tired troops, for whom the morale as well as the physical effects of the bombing were decisive. Secondly, this was one of the rare occasions when Allied bombing fell on a dense concentration of German tanks. (The other incidence was to be the opening of Operation COBRA, when American carpet bombing hit Bayerlein's *Panzer Lehr* Division as it massed to repel an expected advance.)

The RAF bombardment ended, but the respite was brief. Above the dust and smoke of the bombs, the morning mist was clearing to a clear, sunny sky. And high in the blue arrived the 8th United States Air Force. The American formation was very different. Lieutenant Powle of the Household Cavalry looked up from his scout car:

We saw the RAF go in, spread out and low, but the Yanks

A Panzer IV, modified by its crew, and more extensively by the RAF.

came over in tight formations and higher.

An infantryman with 1/Welsh Guards watched from his lorry, on the west bank of the Orne River, near Bénouville:

> *High in the sky and away to our left a faint and steady hum caught our attention and, as we watched, it grew into an insistent throbbing roar and the first aeroplanes appeared high up in the pale sky. Then the whole northern sky was filled with them as far as one could see – wave upon wave, stepped up one above the other.*[6]

Unlike the RAF who were accustomed to flying through the night, more or less individually, in 'streams' of aircraft, the American day bombers favoured tight, mutually supportive formations. An entire American formation would drop its bombs on the signal of its lead aircraft. This produced a more even spread of bombs over the target area, and reduced the advantage of a low-level approach. On this occasion, the American heavies favoured the band between 7,500 and 8,000 feet, above the reach of medium (2cm to 3.7 cm) Flak but below the optimum range of the '88s'. The American heavy bombers had somewhat smaller payloads than the British, and their bomb bays were more subdivided. Their role over GOODWOOD was to cover the areas immediately behind the German front lines with fragmentation bombs, selected to avoid cratering which might impede the tanks' advance.

References

1. *One Chap's War,* diary of Tom Geddes, 1982, p 249-250.
2. *Air Power at the Battlefront*, Ian Gooderson, 1998, ISBN 0-7146-4680-6, also Gooderson's paper Heavy and Medium Bombers in the Close Support Role, Journal of Strategic Studies, vol 15, no 3, September, 1982.
3. *Cross Channel Attack,* Gordon A Harrison, 1950, Library of Congress 51-61669, p 207-208.
4. *The Hardest Victory*, Denis Richards, 1994, ISBN 0-141-39096-4, p 111.
5. French, p 90.
6. Ellis, vol 1, p 174-175.

CHAPTER NINE

TUESDAY, 18 JULY:
11TH ARMOURED DIVISION

Advance to Combat

As the last bombs fell, the 3/Royal Tank Regiment combat group in its tight concentration area prepared to advance, engines already throbbing. For some, final preparation meant a last cigarette in the open air before climbing into to the stifling heat of their armour. On the dot of 07.45 hours the artillery barrage began. Through the haze raised by the bombing, a new line of dust and smoke erupted in the direction of the advance. And some shells fell short. On the right of A Squadron, Buck Kite wondered why some of the tanks ahead of his were suddenly reversing out of the line.

> Then I saw shells were actually dropping on our tanks... We had one or two more casualties from our own guns as we moved forward, then the barrage settled down about 100 yards ahead of us.

Major Bill Close, commander of A Squadron, was watching the crews still exposed outside their tanks when:

> Rrrr, flash, wham! One of our batteries dropped a salvo right among us and a figure dashed over to my tank.
>
> It's Mr Pells, Sir, he's had it!
>
> Philip Pells, 3 Troop Commander, had been caught out of his tank. I told his troop sergeant, Freddie Dale, to take over the troop. He was an experienced sergeant and well able to cope. There were several other casualties, including Major Peter Burr, C Squadron commander, killed.[1]

In spite of the sudden confusion, the tanks had quickly to see to the wounded and get moving in order to keep up with the advancing barrage. Like a fleet raising anchor, 3/Royal Tank Regiment with its supporting arms prepared to move slowly out of harbour and down the newly swept passages through the mines. In 1944, much of the Tank Corps' experience of armoured warfare had been gained amid the entrenchments of the First World War and in the deserts of the North Africa campaign. Prior to GOODWOOD, the experience of combat in Normandy was proving closer to the trenches than the open desert. In the dense terrain of the bocage, movement and ranged fire were narrowly constrained. Now, at last, open country beckoned. The massed British armour lay poised before miles of rippling grain fields, across which it was hoped that the tanks would be able to manoeuvre as squadrons and as whole regiments. Once clear of the narrow lanes, the fleet could shake itself out into battle formation; the tanks could resume the role of land-ships, shrugging off the need for infantry in close support as they swept across the countryside.

The entire force was both mobile and armoured: 'leg' infantry and 'soft skin' vehicles were not to encumber the advance. 3/RTR's A and B Squadrons were to lead, accompanied by infantry of 8/Rifle Brigade. A Squadron formed a 'box' with two troops in front (each of four Shermans, including one Firefly), two behind, and in the middle Close's Headquarters Troop of three tanks. Grinding forward in low gear through the smoke and around the shell holes, the tanks' visibility was limited. They could only trust that, to the left, B Squadron's nineteen tanks, under Jock Balharrie, were moving up alongside in a similar formation. Behind all these, following as closely as the terrain permitted, the second wave included the Colonel, David Silvertop, with his two Sherman headquarters tanks; the twelve Stuart tanks of 3/RTR's Reconnaissance Troop; and, from the attached infantry company of 8/Rifle Brigade, Noel Bell's command vehicle accompanied Silvertop's tank, followed by David Stileman's Carrier Platoon. Also with the colonel in the second wave were a troop of Sherman flail tanks to deal with unexpected minefields, and a half-troop of three AVREs, Churchill tanks manned by Royal Engineers and armed with petard mortars hurling a massive 'Flying Dustbin' bomb containing twenty-three pounds of plastic explosive designed to breach concrete obstacles. Completing the second wave was the regimental anti-aircraft troop of six Crusader tanks, carrying in their turrets twin 20mm Oerlikon guns. The third wave of the regimental group was led by C Squadron's Shermans. Once clear of the mine passages, this squadron divided and raced ahead, two squadrons to each flank of the second wave effectively forming a moving 'box' around the infantry, artillery, and headquarters elements. To the rear of the box followed the rest of the third wave. H Battery of 13/Royal Horse Artillery

The entire force was mobile and armoured.

comprised eight Sexton 25-pounder-armed self-propelled guns with their officers' mounts (Sherman gun-tanks and turretless Stuarts). The remainder of G Company, 8/RB included a dozen infantry-carrying half-tracks, antitank and mortar detachments from the regiment's Support Company, and Noel Bell's G Company headquarters. The multi-arm 'fleet' rolled across the smoking fields of uncut grain.

Even stripped of all 'soft skins' and non-essential support, this regimental group included over 140 armoured vehicles. Among them were the additional recovery vehicles, bulldozers, field ambulances, officers' scout cars, and any unauthorized transport that had evaded the watchful eyes of the Provost Company supervising the one-way traffic flow over the bridges. Behind them, the similarly equipped regimental group of the 2/Fife and Forfarshire Yeomanry prepared to attempt the passage of the minefields, and further back still the 23/Hussars group waited impatiently. Somewhere amongst all these were various divisional vehicles, including batteries of self-propelled

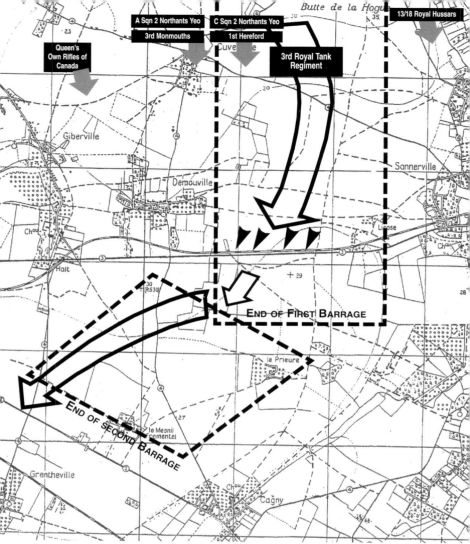

The lead regiment of 11th Armoured advanced with open flanks.

M10s of 75/Antitank Regiment, Roscoe Harvey's 29th Brigade headquarters in command of the three tank regiments, and 'Pip' Roberts' own divisional 'Tac HQ'. On the heels of this cavalcade waited the armoured cars of the Inns of Court Regiment, the 'Devil's Own', who would spend the day aggressively probing for gaps in the enemy line. The scale of the traffic jam that was already building up was disconcerting to a 23/Hussars officer:

For the first time one felt slight misgivings. Would that long tail of supporting arms ever manage to keep up with the leading tanks? One thought of the gaps through the minefield and... even before the minefield had been reached, it looked as if the maintenance of correct distances was not going to be more than a pious hope. If we, as reserve Regiment, were going to be left behind, how much more so were the Guards and the Seventh Armoured.[2]

The going was flat, and for 3/RTR there was some room to manoeuvre. But this was not the desert. The moving armoured box formation was designed to provide flank cover, but equally was designed for traversing wide open spaces. The corridor down which 3/RTR advanced was barely 2,000 yards wide. As the leading tanks skirted the rubble that had been the hamlet of Cuverville, the corridor narrowed still further. The way forward ran between the Démouville wood on the right and the orchards and unsuppressed buildings of Touffreville on the right. (On their own initiative, and without informing 2nd Army, the RAF had moved their bombing line to the south of Touffreville. While intended to reduce the risk of 'friendly fire' casualties, the sparing of this strongpoint was to have unfortunate consequences for the development of the left flank of the British advance.) Still, amid the smoke and confusion, 3/RTR continued to roll forward. Bill Close recalled,

We roared on through boiling clouds of dirt and fumes, thirty eight Shermans [the two leading squadrons] *doing their best to keep up with the rolling curtain of fire. I could vaguely see tanks on either side of me slowly picking their way through the ever-increasing number of bigger and bigger bomb craters... Dazed and shaken figures rose from the uncut corn and attempted to give themselves up to the leading tanks. When I waved them to the rear they stumbled off with their hands over their ears. Other Germans squatted in their foxholes staring stupidly, completely demoralized as we passed. Our infantry would collect them, or so we hoped. Sure enough, we could see David Stileman's carriers rounding them up.*[3]

Behind A Squadron, Jim Caswell

...thought back to our experience of similar bombardments against us in Greece and the early days in the desert after the Afrika Korps arrival, but the Germans were now being paid back with interest.[4]

Third Royal Tanks Leading

It was 3/RTR's great fortune that they passed through the narrowest part of the corridor while visibility was obscured and the Germans on both flanks were still dazed. The antitank guns on either flank, of which there were many, were comfortably within effective range of the advancing Shermans, but were either disabled by the bombardment or manned by crews too dazed to enter the fight. Some of these were physically overrun. Bill Close takes up the story:

> *I now had my squadron more or less in line covering a frontage of about 600 yards. I gave instructions to No 1 Troop Commander Johnny Langdon: 'Sugar 1, move out to your right. Anti-tank guns firing from the orchard area; use your machine-guns to keep their heads down.' I wanted to slow down and deal with them properly but with instructions from the CO to press on we could only 'brass them up'.*[5]

In another A Squadron tank, Sergeant 'Buck' Kite

> *Very early on... found myself looking down the barrel of an SP gun with the crew milling around it but they were so bomb happy they didn't know what day it was. We had orders to go on through and leave them for the infantry to mop up, but that didn't stop us worrying about the beggars recovering and whacking us up the backside.*[6]

These were possibly survivors of the forward battery of *Sturmgeschütz Abteilung 200*, of which we shall hear more later. The whole battery of German self-propelled guns had been caught when the bombing reduced Cuverville to a lunar landscape: aerial photographs taken shortly after would reveal a dusty white expanse of newly turned rubble reflecting the midday sun where the guns had been. Only the battery's armoured command vehicle escaped the devastation. Passing abeam the woods south-east of Cuverville some opposition from an infantry platoon and to two antitank guns was briefly encountered and equally quickly suppressed.[7] The survivors were left to the care of the Herefords of 11th Armoured Division's infantry brigade who were to clear the wood. As ordered, 3/RTR rolled on south.

The first major objective was the Caen-Vimont railway line. This single-track railway lay directly across the tanks' advance, but had been dismissed by APIS (the Aerial Photography Interpretation Section) as an insignificant obstacle. APIS was

The first obstacle: the level crossing west of Lirose (the modern N175) was a useful crossing point. There is now a roadside picnic area by the crossing keeper's house where the Pak 40 crew sabotaged their gun at full recoil.

N

wrong. ('Pip' Roberts later conceded that this was 'the only mistake they made in the campaign.') Fortunately, the Royal Engineers had laid on additional support to meet 'unforeseen needs', travelling directly behind 3/RTR these took the form of a troop of 612 Field Squadron, mounted in half-tracks and with two armoured bulldozers, and ten AVREs of 26 Assault Squadron. Guns emplaced along the tree-lined railway line had been effectively neutralized by the Americans' fragmentation bombs. But the railway across the path of 3/RTR ran atop a hedge-lined embankment between one and two metres high – no serious obstacle for a fully-tracked tank but virtually impassable for the accompanying half-tracks and wheeled vehicles. By 09.00 hours these were crowding around the few level crossings along the stretch of track, waiting to take their turn. Also inconvenienced were the Sherman 'Crab' tanks whose ungainly overhanging flails prevented them from smashing through a hedge-lined bank. Foreseeing the difficulty, Bill Close had the presence of mind to call up the Royal Engineers with their AVREs and demolition charges to begin blasting more gaps through the embankment.

The artillery bombardment was designed to pause briefly at this point before recommencing in front of 3/RTR's new direction, veering right towards the distant Bourguébus ridge. However, word of the traffic jam at the railway crossings got back to 'Pip' Roberts' Tac HQ where the divisional artillery commander tried to extend the pause. His work was interrupted as the enemy began to stir from the shock of the bombing.

> *The CRA was very busy organizing this change when we were quite heavily shelled... so I moved the Tac HQ some 500 yards to the left. No sooner had we settled there than we got "stonked" again, and this time the map-board on which the CRA was doing calculations was cut clean in half by a piece of shell.*[8]

In spite of the efforts of the divisional Commander, Royal Artillery, the barrage moved on before 3/RTR had completed the crossing, but Bill Close's leading squadron shook themselves out into open formation and sped up in pursuit. They soon encountered another obstacle. Less than half a mile to the south, a substantial hedgerow lay in the path of the advance. Again the tanks had to slow down, seeking the few points where less dense undergrowth would permit a tank to

Manneville 'haras'

le Prieuré

The Autoroute de Normandie today marks the line of hedgerows which offered cover from long-range fire. Beyond the hedgerows lay open fields.

charge the earth bank and crash through the foliage. Fortunately, there was still little or no enemy fire as the lead tanks made the attempt, and as time went by a half-dozen crossing points were established. But again the advance was slowed as tanks waited their turn to cross.

With this obstacle behind them, a mile of open ground lay ahead of A Squadron and the leading tanks again sped up to try to catch the artillery bombardment. And now the defenders were beginning to fight back. Shortly after 09.00 hours, the artillery barrage had reached its furthest limit at the farm complex of le Mesnil Frémentel. Infantrymen warily emerged from shelter; gunners began to pull debris and camouflage off antitank guns, clearing their pieces for action. Towards 09.30 hours, as A Squadron crossed open country, concealed guns began to fire from positions directly ahead, in and around the farm. As A Squadron veered westward,

> ...odd rounds of solid shot stared whistling by and it was obviously the first signs of organized resistance. Suddenly a Sherman on my left rolled to a halt belching smoke. Immediately, every tank turned its guns on the houses in the village from where the shot had come.[9]

The tanks' path angled still further westward, away from the sources of the fire, towards another substantial hedgerow running east-west across the line of the advance. This time the hedgerow served not only as an obstacle but also as effective cover. Tanks manoeuvred into positions offering a line of sight through the foliage. But there was no time to stand and fight. Bill Close was unhappy at being told to advance across the face of known German gun positions, but the order was emphatic.

> I wanted to stop and use my squadron properly and put down

a shoot but I was being told by my CO in no uncertain terms to get on, get moving, and go to the west of the village.[10]

Funnelling through the few crossing points into open fields, the tanks emerged one by one, barely a quarter of a mile from the defended farm. The tanks' only protection was their rapid movement across the face of the emplaced German guns, and the residual dust and smoke left hanging in the air by the recent barrage. Until they could gain a dip in the ground west of le Mesnil Frémentel they were in full view, broadside on, at point blank range of the heavy antitank guns. Accurate return fire was out of the question while on the move, although liberal spraying of machine gun bullets into the orchards around the farmstead distracted the German gunners. At least one A Squadron Sherman and two Stuart tanks of the Recce Troop were left burning in the fields. Looking back, Bill Close witnessed B Squadron taking its turn to run the gauntlet, and further Shermans exploding into flame.

Still A Squadron pressed on, down the slope to the next landmark. Ahead lay the second railway crossing, this time the dual track main Caen-Paris line. Although some of its length was raised on an embankment and some lying in a cutting, this line did not represent a serious obstacle. Beyond the railway lay the village of Grentheville, and in between yet another layer of the German defences. In the fields before the village were the

The north wall of le Mensil Frémental strongpoint.

survivors of *Werfer-Brigade 9.* Nominally equipped with 72 six-tubed *Nebelwerfer,* this unit had already suffered from the aerial bombardment, and now was overrun by the tanks; at day's end only twenty-five of the *Werfer* remained operational. As the *Werfer* belched clouds of white smoke and their rockets howled overhead, Bill Close hastily estimated that twenty or thirty gun positions lay ahead, and ordered his squadron to 'brass them up' with machine guns and if necessary to crush them under their tracks. Noel Bell, commanding the accompanying company of 8/Rifle Brigade, observed:

> *Here a 'Moaning Minnie' opened up just in front of us, but before the last of its six barrels had been emptied the turrets of a dozen Shermans swung round and blew it and the crew to pieces – the best thing we had ever seen happen to this diabolical weapon.*[11]

Reaching the enemy's artillery lines would normally signify a breakthrough. Had the second railway line truly marked the German rear defences, the GOODWOOD plan would have been vindicated and a breakthrough achieved before midday on day one. It was not to be. Even as the hapless German artillerymen were overrun, Close could see antitank guns further south, around the village of Grentheville, frantically turning to meet the threat.

> *As I reached a little cornfield a few hundred yards from Grentheville we were engaged by antitank guns on the forward edge of the village. And some of the tanks in my troops on the left, about four of them, went up in flames. I could also see several of the tanks further left, in the left-hand squadron, were also brewing. There was quite a lot of AP shot coming from the bushes and trees in Grentheville and also where the farm buildings are. Obviously antitank guns in very well concealed positions. And within a matter of moments there were five or six tanks brewing up. I told my two right hand troops to tuck themselves down along the line of the embankment and get some HE fire on the forward edges of the village as quickly as possible. I had an OP with me right from the start. He was in a sawn-off Honey and I had given him instructions to stick close to me. I tucked myself in behind a small ridge, called him over, and told him, 'For Christ's sake get a stonk down on as quickly as possible.' All this time, I was being told in no uncertain manner by my CO to get over to the west side of the embankment. And*

I said wait out until I can get a stonk down on the village.[12]

Now beyond the range of the Field Regiments that had laid on the barrage, the only artillery available to 3/RTR was H Battery, 13/Royal Horse Artillery, whose Sextons had followed the tanks' advance. Responding to their officer's call, the eight Sextons' 25-pounder guns quickly began to play on the village, offering some relief. Meanwhile, A Squadron's two right hand troops found what cover they could and rained High Explosive down on the suspected gun positions; they claimed to have knocked out two or three antitank guns and at least one assault gun. But the two left-hand troops of A Squadron and the tanks of B Squadron now appearing on their left were exposed. Once again the tanks were caught at virtually point-blank range, lacking solid cover, seeking shelter in folds of ground and behind foliage. As the morning wore on, Sherman tanks of both A Squadron and B Squadron erupted into flames, while the tiny hamlet of Grentheville stood squarely in 3/RTR's path.

Desperate to get the attack rolling forward, Colonel Silvertop ordered Close to lead his squadron across yet another railway.

The single-track line serving the Colombelles metal works ran due north from the Bourguébus ridge, at right angles to the lines previously crossed. From Bourguébus to Giberville, this line ran on a high, steep-sided embankment, broken only by a dozen underpasses where the line crossed roads, railways, and waterways. These tunnels provided shelter for men of both sides in the course of the battle. The embankment effectively divided the battlefield in two parts thereby blocking lines of sight and fire from one side to the other. A tank might – with extreme difficulty – scale the steep sides, but in so doing would be highly conspicuous and would expose its thinly armoured belly as it crested the slope. For other vehicles, the tunnels were the only crossing points.

From his tank turret, Bill Close

...could see that the embankment was going to be rather a difficult problem, and I did not like the idea of going over the top, broadside on, within a few hundred yards of antitank guns... I wanted to get my two right-hand troops to the western side of the embankment before I followed with the regimental group behind me. So, I gave the order for them to move. Not a tank moved. Nothing happened at all.[13]

Years later, 'Pip' Roberts used this event as an illustration how

Under the railway embankment west of Giberville: in1944 a German aid post, today entrance to a country park.

years of battle experience can make men 'canny'. As a former member and commander of the regiment, with the greatest respect for its achievements, Roberts was uniquely placed to make an objective assessment:

> I don't believe that this would have happened in either of the other three [armoured] regiments in the division. The fact is that with a great deal of fighting, all those concerned become a little more wary and a little more canny. It's more difficult to get people to go 'round the corner' after that sort of experience than it is right at the outset of a campaign.[14]

So it was that, instead of following his leading troops, Bill Close

The rail embankment: a typical bridge west of Grentheville.

had to stand up in his turret and wave his beret in the air, preparatory to his order over the radio *'Conform to me!'* Then, without a backward glance but with very mixed feelings and unsure what to expect, he took his tank forward towards the wide tunnel by which the dual-track Paris railway passed under the single-track embankment. The thought that such a passage would be a likely spot to encounter antitank mines occurred too late, and the tank shot through the gap, unscathed, 'rather like a rat up a drainpipe'.

Alone at the forefront of the VIII Corps advance, Close's tank

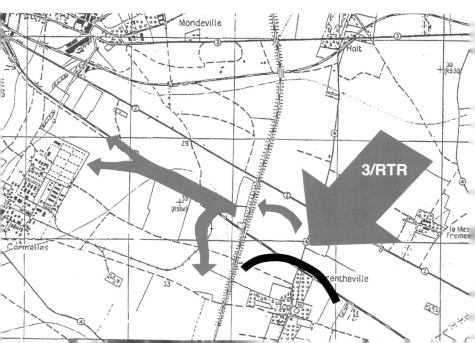

emerged from the tunnel to behold a vista of tranquillity.

> *I emerged on the other side to see this beautiful country looking perfectly peaceful. There was no sign of any movement whatsoever. And I was an extremely relieved squadron commander, I can tell you.*[15]

The dust and smoke of battle was left behind on the east side of the embankment. It was now 11.00 hours and the sun shone down on fields of ripening grain, rippling in the northerly breeze. The high railway embankment ran arrow-straight to the south, disappearing over the distant ridge near the village of Bourguébus. From Close's vantage point, the landscape was dominated by the ridgeline, two miles distant. On its crest to the west of the railway could be seen the church tower and roofs of Hubert Folie, and further west along the ridge a cluster of trees indicated the position of the regimental objective of Bras. Close and his squadron moved due west, keeping the ridge under constant observation. There was no sign of the enemy. Hopes rose that the day's objective, the Bourguébus ridge, might be achievable after all.

Second In: The Fife and Forfars

Emerging from the minefields' swept lanes, the 2/Fife & Forfarshire Yeomanry shook out into a formation similar to the preceding Royal Tanks'. This was a novel experience. The Fifes' first month of combat had so far been spent in dense country around the Odon valley, where tanks would typically scurry in ones and twos from cover to cover. 'We had never before driven in formation for more than a couple of hundred yards, except on exercises,' Steel Brownlie reflected.

Certainly, this was to be a battle different from any that had gone before. The order was:

> *Head for Falaise. Don't stop for anything. When you come across enemy antitank guns, drive at them, destroy them, run over their traces!*
>
> *("Some hopes!"* thought Jack Thorpe, C Squadron, *"What 'nana made that last statement?")*[16]

B Squadron led, along with the Stuart tanks of the Recce Troop. Next came C Squadron, with the Colonel, A J B Scott; and A Squadron brought up the rear. Like 3/RTR before them, the Fifes maintained their box formation as they motored on through the murk. Dazed prisoners sent to the rear by 3/RTR ambled past, still more were emerging from their entrenchments:

> *A few Germans are now climbing out of their foxholes in the ground, obviously shaken, their faces ashen grey as their uniforms, and come towards us with their hands in the air, or resting on the top of their helmets. A man in battle experiences more terror than the average person does in a whole lifetime. We have no means of dealing with prisoners and our tank commander looks down from the top of his turret and, pointing to the rear, shouts to them 'Snell, go back that way'.*

Still there was no threat. The tank men had time to think about what lay ahead.

'We are all keyed up,' reflected Jack Thorpe in the front of his Sherman,

> *...as this is equivalent to 'going over the top'. I know I'm scared... you feel you want to screw yourself up into the tiniest space, smaller than you are, you are alone with fear a pain in the back of your head and your body cold and frozen. Now breathing in gasps, you pass through your fear – it is almost like getting your second wind when you are running! The crashing shells of the barrage help to settle us down to the task in hand.*

Fear was not the only discomfort:

> *There is a huge pall of smoke and dust drifting across the sky, but it's going to be a hot day. When the sun beats down, the metal of our tanks becomes black hot and you cannot touch the outside with bare skin and, when the tanks stop moving, it becomes a sweltering oven inside. Most of our boys are suffering from a form of dysentery* [for once, the chloride of lime added to the bowsers had failed to deal with something putrid in the regimental water supply] *and most of them have already had to get down to relieve themselves. We are all dehydrated... Now, a number of tanks are making limited stops and the crews are seen to be squatting behind their tanks before getting back and trying to catch up.*

The Fifes' start had been delayed; they had been unable to make up time in the initial advance; now as the first railway line was reached B Squadron ran into the back of the traffic jam of 3/RTR vehicles queuing at the level crossings. As diarrhoea sufferers took the welcome opportunity to clean up, a wireless signal came through ordering the Fifes to take down their cap badges to avoid them glinting in the sun and giving away the tanks' positions. With reluctance, regret, and annoyance in equal measure the tankers removed the metal badges from their berets.

What a laugh! Anyone on the enemy side who is the least bit organized knows we are here!

Clear of the rail line, the regimental formation spread out, angling south-west in the path of 3/RTR, but on approaching le Mesnil Frémentel the regiments' paths diverged. After the last squadron of 3/RTR made its run past le Mesnil Frémentel, urged on by their impatient Colonel Silvertop, Brigadier Roscoe Harvey arrived with his 29th Brigade Tactical Headquarters group and shortly after began to organize the assault on the farm's defences. Arriving on the scene, 8/Rifle Brigade's Headquarters group with elements of E (Support) Company were to lead the attack, covered by the guns of 75/Antitank Regiment's 199 Battery (self-propelled M10s with seventeen pounder guns) and to the west by the 22/Dragoons' Sherman Crabs which 'Pip' Roberts had not wanted in the battle. As predicted by Roberts, the flails mineclearing role had so far not been needed, and the unwieldy tanks had fallen behind the lead regiment, but their 75mm guns provided welcome support to the infantry. Under cover of the tanks' fire, Rifle Brigade carriers swept through the cornfields, machine guns blazing to keep defenders' heads down. Close behind came a motor infantry platoon with an armoured 'Dingo' scout car and three half-tracks. These drove alongside the western wall of le Mesnil Frémentel, where the infantry disembarked and began the lengthy process of clearing the defenders.

Le Mesnil: the west wall over which the 8/RB attack went in.

The Fifes departed from the tracks left by 3/RTR, turning south to pass le Mesnil Frémentel on their right. As the leading squadrons went by, the guns of the farm complex were effectively suppressed. Becker's *4. Batterie* had briefly opposed 3/RTR from positions in the vicinity but now, in accordance with Becker's successful tactics of keeping his vulnerable batteries at arm's length, had now fallen back before the tide of British armour to take up positions in and around the farm complex of le Poirier. Several accounts of GOODWOOD[17] suggest that Becker's *4. Batterie* remained around le Mesnil Frémentel as late as 11.00 hours. This is barely credible. The route taken by the battery's withdrawing guns ran directly across the path which the Fifes were to take from 09.30 hours onwards. By 10.00 hours there was no escape route open to the south, and the Germans who conducted the last defence of the farm had no armour in support. Also, the battery appears to have been established at le Poirier not much later than 10.00 hours.[18]

Crossing the main Cagny-Caen road, the Fifes' B Squadron led the way towards the second railway. A Squadron had by this time overtaken C, and passing le Mesnil Frémentel, their attention was also directed forward, towards the railway. So far, the Fifes' regimental history recorded, their battle had been *'as easy as a coach trip'*.[19] Steel Brownlie wondered, *'Was it all over bar the shouting?'* By 10.00 hours, 3/RTR and 2/F&F each had two squadrons across the Paris railway line and more following. But the tide of battle was about to turn.

Emerging from the smoke and dust of the barrage the Fife & Forfar crews began to be aware of enemy activity. Both B and A Squadrons became conscious of their exposed position. Steel

N

From around the le Prieuré farm complex, German gunners enjoyed an open view across the armoured corridor.

Brownlie saw friendly tanks brewing; he shot at some enemy infantry and some but not all ran away; mortar bombs began falling around his troop:

> *A Squadron's immediate objective was the second railway line, and we got across its high embankments one way or another.* [The railway was flanked in places by substantial hedgerows. See page 154.] *My 4 Troop and the Third-in-Command, Pinkie Hutchinson, were given the job of looking left and covering that flank, while the rest of the regiment* [actually, the rest of A Squadron] *went on, down into the valley in front. We had no cover, except for the shape of the ground, and simply sat in the corn.*[20]

Ahead lay open fields, sloping gently upwards. The way ahead resembled a half-saucer, with the Fifes in the bowl. Higher up was a ring of ominous clumps of stone buildings: Frénouville, le Poirier, Four, Soliers. The farmsteads and small villages were evenly spaced at intervals of about a thousand yards, ideal antitank range. And behind these, on the saucer's rim, loomed the Bourguébus ridge from which armoured vehicles were already descending the slopes to meet the British advance.

The Fate of 'C' Squadron

A mile to the rear, the Fifes' C Squadron had begun to experience opposition from the left flank of the armoured corridor. In the co-driver's seat of the sergeant's tank of 4 Troop, Jack Thorpe's eyes were glued to his periscope:

> *There are little copses lining the valley about 400 yards away from us each side.* [Several accounts refer to the armoured corridor as a 'valley'; this impression was created by the distant higher ground of the Bois de Bavent to the east.] *We*

know there is no cover but it is necessary to follow the leading tanks in the column. Now the crack of high velocity armour piercing shots are passing over us. 88s! We are committed, there is nowhere to take cover, we are sitting ducks! Still moving forward, Cliff directs our gunner to take aim at a copse slightly to our left, and, when ready, to fire first one AP round, followed by an HE round, and carry on at will. The tank turns towards the copse and I get the order to train my Browning machine gun onto the same copse and to keep firing because Cliff thinks that we have met up with an anti-tank battery.

Sergeant Clifford Jones was right. Guns that had remained quiet as the earlier squadrons had passed were now coming into action, with devastating results. After lengthy sustained fire, Jack Thorpe's Browning jammed as the canvas bag collecting spent cartridges filled and blocked the ejector:

I had never before needed to keep firing so long. I rip off the stupid small bag and, in disgust, fling it down on the floor where it can do no more harm. (The Americans are supposed to think big, they have made these tanks for a one-day picnic, never supposing they would be fought in day after day and lived in for days on end. I consider they were made like aeroplanes, for single sorties!) I load my gun and commenced to fire again... I feed in one belt after another and my gun begins to warp as the barrel gets red hot and I see the tracer leaving the gun in a spray-cone... Cliff is still standing in the turret giving instructions and directions and the tank is slowly advancing... All bloody go, the gun ammunition is running out in the turret and Bert is calling for me to pass up the rounds from the rack behind me.

The fate of C Squadron is recorded by its few survivors. Departing from the tracks left by A and B, C Squadron edged left to 'mask' the village of Cagny. Crossing a triangular field between le Mesnil Frémentel and Cagny, the squadron was taken in the flank by volleys of antitank fire. Through Jack Thorpe's periscope,

...along the column of tanks, I see palls of smoke and tanks brewing up with flames belching forth from their turrets. I see men climbing out, on fire like torches, rolling on the ground to try and douse the flames, but we are in ripe corn and the straw takes fire. Soon, what with the burning tanks and the burning men and the burning cornfield, plus smoke shells and smoke mortar shells from our tank, visibility is being shut out. Now

every tank I can see in front of me is brewing, burning fiercely, flames shooting high and dense clouds of smoke rising up. The tank twenty yards away from us is hit, flames shoot out of its turret, I see a member of its crew climbing out through the flames, he is almost out, putting one foot onto the rim to jump down, he seems to hesitate and he falls back inside. Oh Christ!

The majority of C Squadron's tanks were knocked out. Those immobilized tanks that failed to burn were hard to distinguish from those few still manned, and continued to be hit over and over as the German gunners ran out of live targets.

Cliff orders Bert to fire off more smoke shells and tells Robbie to reverse, and we go backwards, zig-zagging, right stick, left stick, right stick, gunner keep on target and keep firing, left stick, right stick, left stick.

Finally reaching cover in a hull-down position the crew took stock.

We have used up most of our gun ammunition. We have lost wireless contact with the rest of the Regiment - we cannot raise our Troop Leader, nor the Squadron Leader or the CO.

In fact, the tank of the Squadron commander Major Chris Nicholl was the first to be knocked out, and a moment later Captain Miller's was likewise destroyed. Four C Squadron tanks survived the massacre. Jack Thorpe's tank reversed all the way to the first railway line, where they found the 23/Hussars' advance stalled by concentrated antitank fire from the vicinity of le Prieuré. Not knowing the fate of their squadron or their regiment, they tagged along with the Hussars. Another survivor was Trooper John Brown, driving a Firefly which had been further forward when the execution commenced. The tank pressed on forward, away from the carnage, its turret traversed and its gun firing backwards on the move. When the order to bale out came, Brown found his hatch jammed by the traversed turret and so he squeezed sideways over the ammunition racks to escape through the adjacent co-driver's hatch:

Lying beside the tank, we realised that it was only our equipment and bedding on the hull that was burning. Pulling this off I said that I would get back into the tank and bring it into the shelter of the house at the level crossing. I had got in and started the engine when suddenly a horrible eruption of molten metal came in through the side immediately behind the ammunition, like an acetylene cutter in action. I was able to bale out faster than the first time.

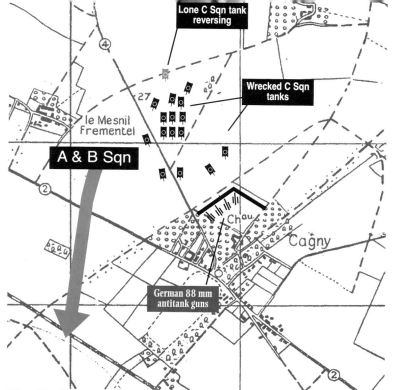

The Cauldron of Four

The Fifes' B Squadron led the way into the open fields beyond the second railway line. As if to a signal, unseen batteries suddenly opened up, raking the lines of Sherman tanks. The closer the tanks' approach to the orchard-fringed hamlet of Four, the more ferocious became the defenders' fire. The colonel's tank was knocked out, then the second-in-command. The tanks were being shattered as quickly as the German gunners could reload. As the advance ground to a halt, the third-in-command Captain 'Pinkie' Hutchinson attempted a flanking manoeuvre with two troops of A Squadron. Leading one of these troops, on the Fifes' extreme left flank, Steel Brownlie records the close-quarters scrap that ensued, ranges closing to mere hundreds of yards as the smoke of battle spread arose the landscape:

I was at once fired on by what appeared to be a self-propelled gun in the valley, and two tanks to the right of me went up in smoke. To the southeast was an artillery position, a row of guns, maybe 105mms. [Possibly these were some of the eighteen

123

12.2cm Russian guns of 1255.s.Heeres.Küsten Artillerie Abteilung deployed around le Poirier.] *They were firing. I did an HE shoot on them, until they shut up, and there was no movement except wisps of smoke. A Panther came at full pelt past their position and into the village on our left* [this would have been the farm complex of le Poirier, where Becker's battery from le Mesnil Frémentel was installed] *It poked its nose out of the edge of the trees, and one of its crew got out and started to camouflage it with branches. My Charlie tank brewed it with its 17 Pdr. Meanwhile all kinds of things were going on down in the valley, beyond our sight...*

Down in the valley Ron Cox, wireless operator in the troop sergeant's Sherman,

...realised for the first time that things were going badly for us when I saw through the periscope that the tank of our troop leader, Lieutenant Miller, had gone up in flames. No one got out. Sergeant Herd remained quite calm. "Driver reverse!" he ordered. Then, 'Halt!' He kept repeating those two commands, hoping to get back to cover. The tank shuddered and stopped. 'Track broken; we've been hit.' It was Charlie's voice over the intercom. Still calm, Willy Herd gave the order to traverse the gun. It had been blocking Charlie's escape hatch. Then, 'Bale out!'.

As tank after tank succumbed, stricken crews began to make their way back to safety, passing Steel Brownlie's position. Bedraggled and singed tankers limping back from the battle were a recurring theme throughout the afternoon of 18 July:

Burnt and injured men kept coming back through the corn. We gave them a drink of water, and told them to keep going. Sometimes we tried first-aid. Some were walking, some crawling.

A self-propelled gun was engaged and knocked out, but then Panther tanks began to appear in the gloom and,

...things got really warm... We wished we had gunner support here, but the guns were too far behind by now.

In fact, the eight attached Sexton guns of 'I' Battery, 13/Royal Horse Artillery were struggling forward, around the west side of le Mesnil Frémentel, to take up firing positions by the Paris rail line, but could do little by way of direct support for the tanks locked in a close-quarters mêlée around Four. About midday, Steel Brownlie ran out of ammunition and replenished

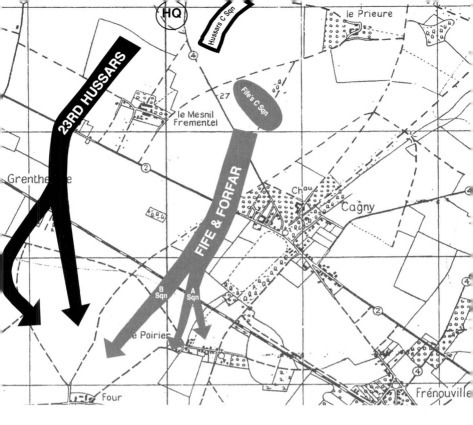

from a tank that had not brewed up. Later, the two Brownings'
barrels were thoroughly worn out, and were likewise replaced
from an immobilized wreck. So the struggle continued, tanks
and self-propelled guns milling in the smoke, desperate short-
range encounters flaring as the Fifes' hopes of reaching the
distant ridgeline diminished along with the numbers of their
surviving tanks.

The Hussars' Progress

After frustrating delays, the 23/Hussars finally entered the
lanes through the minefields,

> ...clearly marked with white tape, but so narrow that vehicles
> had to pass down the lanes in single file.

Emerging on the far side, the regiment faced a difficult decision:
to attempt to regain the precise formation planned, or to press
on regardless. As a compromise,

> We paused for a moment to get back into our formation, but

Destroyed Russian artillery piece (stripped of its wheels by French farmers).

by the time we were all assembled and ready to move forward, the leading regiments were one mile in front of us instead of three hundred yards.[21]

Like the two preceding regiments, the Hussars found the early stages of the journey down the corridor easy enough. The German survivors of the bombing were still white and stunned; for every one trying to surrender there seemed to be half a dozen sitting dazed in their entrenchments. Soon after 09.30 hours, the first railway was reached. Now evidence of the fighting ahead was all too plain, as:

Sad little parties began to come back on foot. They were the surviving members of the leading crews, and obviously there had been some trouble. They all looked smoke grimed, as does anyone who has just jumped out of a burning tank, while beside the more active members staggered the black-skinned figures of badly burned men. Some of the parties carried stretchers, on which still figures lay.

The corridor beyond the first railway was no longer an easy passage. The guns that had so recently massacred C Squadron of the Fife and Forfars awaited new targets, and before long the left hand C Squadron of the Hussars was taking losses. Shortly before 10.00 hours, the survivors of Becker's *5. Batterie* disengaged from their positions around the le Prieuré farm, the guns taking a clockwise route around Cagny and Frénouville, passing behind *4. Batterie* now located in le Poirier, and on to take up new defensive positions at Four. A troop of Hussars probing east in their wake past le Prieuré ran straight into advancing Tiger tanks. 8.8cm guns roared. Many of the German shots went wide of their mark, but two Shermans were squarely hit, one having its turret blown clean off. The Hussars moved on south, carefully skirting the killing fields around Cagny; their A Squadron lingered as a rearguard, 'screening' against any German advance out of Cagny until the lead elements of Guards Armoured Division should arrive on the scene. Captain L G Heywood of the Grenadier Guards who had been attached to the Hussars as divisional liaison officer now hastened back to his regiment to bring on its foremost squadron of tanks.

Command and Control

Meanwhile, an event had taken place which was to have untold consequences for the outcome of the GOODWOOD battle. Soon after the ambush and massacre of the Fife & Forfars' C Squadron, Lieutenant Colonel Alec Scott became aware that his rear squadron had gone off the air. Looking back at columns of smoke rising from their last known positions, it was quickly evident that something disastrous had occurred, and the source of the disaster was doubtless to be found in Cagny. Scott immediately ordered his accompanying motor infantry, F Company of 8/Rifle Brigade, to prepare to move on Cagny to remove the threat.

At the same time, 'Pip' Roberts' divisional Tac HQ had just moved up to join Roscoe Harvey's 29th Brigade HQ group, sheltering behind the major hedgerow north of le Mesnil Frémentel. Dodging incoming mortar rounds, Roberts got up onto the back of Harvey's tank to get the brigadier's appreciation of the situation. Things seemed to be going to plan. German artillery and mortar fire was beginning to be a major nuisance. But most importantly 3/RTR and 2/Fifes were pushing on undeterred towards their objectives, and the Hussars were coming up behind. Le Mesnil Frémentel was being subdued by HQ Company, 8/Rifle Brigade supported by the unwanted flail tanks, leaving the tank regiments to press on. True, 159th Infantry Brigade along with 151/Field Regiment's guns (the Ayrshire Yeomanry) and the Cromwells of

2/Northants Yeomanry were still back in the rear clearing Démouville, but this was expected.

Then, Roberts overheard on Harvey's radio the preparations being made by F Company, 8/RB to take Cagny.

I heard that it was the intention of the CO of the Fife and Forfar Yeomanry to get his motor company on their feet and to attack Cagny. Bearing in mind that I had particularly asked that we should not have to take Cagny, and bearing in mind that our objectives were further over on the right flank, I did not want to start getting involved on the left flank, as the Guards were coming forward and they were going to take over Cagny. So, I told Brigadier Harvey to cancel that order.[22]

In later years, Roberts was to reflect how unfortunate was this cancellation. With hindsight it was clear that the company could easily have cleared the village, allowing Guards Armoured Division to pass through and (possibly) unhinge the German defensive line. As it was, Roberts personally briefed the first Guards tanks he encountered, warning their CO that Cagny was strongly held. His well-intentioned warning was heeded, adding to their caution. Roberts was later to admit, '*I fear I badly misled them.*'[23] But on this day the fog of war and the heat of battle were to lead to lost opportunities on both sides.

References

1. Close, p 117.
2. Bishop, p 72.
3. Close, p 118.
4. Caswell diary.
5. Close, p 118.
6. *Panzer Bait*, William Moore, 1991, ISBN 0 85052 3281, p 142.
7. Jackson, p 94.
8. *From the Desert to the Baltic*, Major General G P B Roberts, 1987, ISBN 0-7183-0639-2, p 173.
9. Close, p 121.
10. Close, interview at Staff College, Camberley, 1979.
11. *From the Beaches to the Baltic*, Noel Bell, 1947, p 27.
12. Close, interview at Staff College, Camberley, 1979.
13. Close, interview at Staff College, Camberley, 1979.
14. Roberts, interview at Staff College, Camberley, 1979.
15. Close, interview at Staff College, Camberley, 1979.
16. This and other extracts from Thorpe diary.
17. *Mounting the Threat*, John Sweet, 1977, Library of Congress 77-073555, p 85.
18. GOODWOOD, Lt A G Heywood, Household Brigade Magazine, Winter 1956-57, p 175.
19. *The Fife and Forfar Yeomanry*, R J B Sellar, 1960, p 167.
20. Steel Brownlie diary.
21. Bishop, p 72.
22. Roberts, interview at Staff College, Camberley, 1979.
23. Roberts, p 175.

CHAPTER TEN

TUESDAY, 18 JULY:
21. PANZERDIVISION

Von Luck's Return

It was the good fortune of *21. Panzerdivision* that one of its key officers missed the shocking ordeal of the aerial bombardment but returned to his unit in time to reorganize in the face of the Allied onslaught. Von Luck's story has often been told, with varying details, but is recounted here in as precise form as can be ascertained.

In the afternoon of 14 July, Major von Luck had been summoned by his friend *SS Obergruppenführer* 'Sepp' Dietrich. Arriving, he found Feuchtinger present, and was informed that his divisional commander had recommended him for the *Ritterkreuz* (Knight's Cross of the Iron Cross). Knowing that 15 July was von Luck's birthday, and aware that his fiancée (whose ancestry prevented her marrying a serving officer) was lodged in Paris, Dietrich and Feuchtinger persuaded von Luck to take two days' leave in the capital. After an enjoyable rest, von Luck left Paris in the early hours of 18 July in order to complete most of the return journey under cover of darkness. Reassured by daily telephone calls to his unit that all was quiet, von Luck had

Major von Luck (still wearing his 'little pistol') was briefed as to the situation upon his return from Paris.

no reason to suspect anything amiss. As dawn broke and he neared the combat zone, he noted a haze in the air ahead, but nothing to be concerned about. He arrived at his Frénouville headquarters around 09.00 hours, still looking forward to a good breakfast, following which he would change out of his dress uniform and resume work.

Von Luck was met by his *I. Bataillon* commander, *Hauptmann* Schenk zu Schweinsburg, with the news that 'thousands' of bombers had been attacking the regiment, and that all communications with the forward troops were cut. How was his battalion? *II. Bataillon*? Becker's assault guns?

It was clear that nothing had been done... Nothing, nothing at all had been done! My deputy appeared to be in shock. He seemed absolutely helpless.[1]

Himself a combat veteran, von Luck reacted with disgust at the apathy around him (Schweinsburg was soon relieved of command). Von Luck immediately ordered his adjutant to send out despatch riders to his own *II. Bataillon* and the *Panzer* units to the north, and to restore contact with divisional headquarters. Then, without breakfast and still in his dress uniform, he summoned the *Befehlspanzer IV* (command tank) put at his disposal by *22. Panzerregiment*. Offering the driver a cigarette, he ordered him to drive along the main Caen road towards the *I. Bataillon* headquarters at le Mesnil Frémentel. Cagny had been half destroyed. Then, rounding the southwestern corner of the little town, von Luck was horrified by the sight of dozens of British tanks streaming past. Fifty, perhaps sixty[2] were already across the main road and approaching the Caen-Paris rail line. It was clearly impossible to reach le Mesnil Frémentel. At best, *I. Bataillon* was isolated; at worst it might already have been overwhelmed, in which case there was a gaping hole in the German defences. With division, *II. Bataillon*, and the *Panzer* units still not responding to radio calls, von Luck's only recourse was to return to headquarters to patch up a new defence line and – if possible – organize counter-attacks.

The command tank crept back around the rubble of Cagny. Above a wall, von Luck spotted the barrel of a single cannon, pointing skywards. He dismounted to investigate and found, in a patch of ground untouched by the bombing, a battery of four 8.8cm antiaircraft guns manned by *Luftwaffe* crews:

I went over to the CO and informed him about what I had

A *Luftwaffe* 8.8cm flak crew take a break during the Normandy fighting.

seen. And I gave a clear order to get immediately involved in this battle by fighting the British tanks. But, I got a flat refusal telling me that he was under air command and had nothing to do with our battle on the ground.

The young *Hauptmann* was perfectly within his rights to respond in this way: not only were the loyalties of the German armed forces split between their leaders' 'private armies' (*Himmler's SS*, Goering's *Luftwaffe*), but also the Flak units' doctrine put antitank action at a lower priority than air defence. Von Rosen thought otherwise:

So, I took my little pistol [the small sidearm mandatory with dress uniform for self defence in Paris] *and asked him whether he would like to be killed immediately or get a high decoration. He decided for the latter. So, he got a clear order to get in position with his battery at the north west corner of Cagny, not to deal with the advancing tanks but with the following tanks coming from the north east.*[3]

The battery did not have far to move. But exchanging a walled orchard for a field a short way to the north opened up a vista right across the British armoured corridor, an arc of fire from le Mesnil Frémentel in the west to le Prieuré to the north. Nor was the battery long idle. No sooner were the guns unhooked in their new firing positions than C Squadron of the Fife & Forfars

N

le Prieuré

Field of fire of the Cagny guns: North-west to le Prieuré (above); north along the 'ruisseau' to Manneville (right).

Manneville

obligingly arrived, at point blank range, in fulfilment of their mission to 'screen' Cagny's western flank. The guns fired until they ran out of targets, then with the immediate enemy disposed of, they looked further afield for new prey.

Reorganization

Von Luck's worst-case scenario was not far from the mark. The infantry screen of 16. *Luftwaffenfelddivision* had been shattered, with only the bravest of isolated outposts and guns putting up a fight. To the west, his sister *192. Regiment* risked being overrun. No news came back from them during the day, and only in the evening was a do-or-die radio message of farewell received at Feuchtinger's headquarters from the regiment's second battalion: 'surrounded in Mondeville – fighting to the last – long live the Führer – Sieg Heil!' (The heroic effect was somewhat spoiled when the commander *Hauptmann* Rusche had second thoughts and turned up at divisional headquarters later in the night. Division were 'surprised' but glad of the unexpected reinforcement.) Of von Luck's own *125. Regiment*, the first battalion was indeed cut off at le Mesnil Frémentel, though unbeknown to him still fighting. North of Cagny, the silence of the *Panzer* units was ominous. For all his exhortations to the young *Hauptmann* of the *Luftwaffe*, von Rosen felt that Cagny was likely to be untenable. He was not yet prepared to invest any of his precious infantry in its defence.

Nevertheless, von Luck arrived back at his Frénouville command post to welcome news. Contact had been restored with both his second battalion and his commander. The former was upbeat. *Major* Kurz was already pulling together the defenders of Emiéville and Cuillerville, and confidant that he could build a west-facing stop line. Von Luck's adjutant, *Hauptmann* Liebeskind, brought less welcome news from division. Though praising von Luck's initiative, Feuchtinger could not yet release any substantial reinforcements. Though von Luck saw that his left flank was wide open to any attack along the axis Cagny-Vimont, Feuchtinger maintained that the divisional reconnaissance and pioneer battalions were still required on the Bourguébus ridge as a protective screen for the divisional antitank battalion. (Note that all these units were in positions which the British had believed to be far behind the rearmost enemy lines.) For now, von Luck had only his second infantry battalion, and the surviving batteries of *Major* Becker.

Becker was a pillar of support. Arriving at the Frénouville command post, he was able to give a full account of his unit, due to the unique low-frequency radios which linked his companies (and were not subject to Allied eavesdropping). Furthest forward, *1. Batterie* had been wiped out. Its antitank guns in Cuverville and howitzers around Démouville were reported lost by *Hauptmann* Eichorn, whose armoured command vehicle was the sole survivor of the battery. Eichorn continued to report as a huge tide of British tanks swept southwards past his concealed position. *2. Batterie* in Giberville had missed the worst of the bombardment, and offered fire support to surviving infantry elements before retiring west through tunnels under the railway embankment and onward to positions north-west of Bras, from which they would later deliver flanking fire against 3/RTR's advance up the ridge. *3. Batterie* remained firmly established around Grentheville, blocking the path of 3/RTR.

Becker's *4. Batterie* had briefly resisted at le Mesnil Frémentel before slipping away to avoid the isolation which awaited the infantry garrison, and was now en route to new positions at le Poirier. Meanwhile *5. Batterie* around the walled farmstead of le Prieuré continued to shore up the eastern neck of the corridor while defences were reorganized in the woods behind; with these in place the surviving guns would displace south to positions around Four. How many of Becker's guns were lost by midday on 18 July may never be known. Becker's own claim of no losses apart from *1. Batterie* is disproved by ample photographic evidence of the wrecks of his guns on various parts of the battlefield. Nevertheless, the morale support these guns gave to the defenders in the early stages of the battle can not be overemphasized. For von Luck, to whom had fallen the defence of the eastern half of the battlefield, Becker's batteries were vital, his only mobile tactical resource.[4]

From this point, von Luck's situation changed for the better. As the shock of the aerial bombardment wore off, the defensive line between Frénouville and Emiéville was gradually restored. Further north, beyond the area of Von Luck's responsibility, other infantry and antitank units doggedly defended the wood-shrouded Bois de Bavent against the left-flank British 3rd Infantry Division. Best of all, from von Luck's point of view, there had still been no British breakthrough at Cagny. He

Two views of a *2.Batterie* **7.5 cm gun disabled in Giberville; a second was destroyed across the road.**

reconnoitred forward, again in his command tank, this time more cautiously. Once again, the sight that met his eyes on arriving back in Cagny took his breath away. Where before there had been wave after wave of British tanks passing south, now he found,

> ...at least forty British tanks, on fire or shot up. I saw how the tanks that had already crossed the main road were slowly rolling back.[5]

How the four guns had survived without any infantry

A 10.5 cm Pzkw 38H (f) destroyed in open ground west of Touffreville.

protection was a mystery. Nevertheless, congratulating the young *Luftwaffe Hauptmann*, von Luck ordered him to hold in place as long as possible, promising him a section of infantry to help secure the position. Then von Luck returned quickly to Frénouville to pass the welcome news to Feuchtinger:

> *General, I believe that the whole British attack has come to a standstill... but I see a great danger however on my right wing. If the British were to move up their infantry things would look pretty bad for my rather thin defensive front.*

Feuchtinger was of course delighted, and was now able to offer not only encouragement but also practical help. By afternoon, the lead elements of *1. SS-Panzerdivision*, the *'Leibstandarte'*, began to appear on the southern edge of the battlefield, allowing Feuchtinger at last to release his reconnaissance regiment, Brandt's *21. Panzer-Aufkärungsabteilung*, to von Luck, who in turn sent Brandt's infantry forward to shore up his precarious line.

With his general's warm praise ringing in his ears, and knowing that *12. SS-Panzerdivision 'Hitler Jugend'* would arrive to take over his sector at nightfall, von Luck at last took time to change out of his dress uniform.

Counter-attack

1944 heavy bombers were inefficient battlefield weapons. The tactics of RAF Bomber Command were designed for the destruction of urban areas, where their ability consistently to place ninety percent of bombs dropped within a one thousand-yard radius was highly effective.[6] But military targets in the open were usually far too dispersed to make such precision desirable. GOODWOOD was a rare exception. The *Panzer* units around Emiéville were caught squarely in the bomb pattern. Emiéville itself ceased to exist. Roads and stone buildings merged in a sea of rubble. Of the fifty or so *Panzer IV* of *Panzerregiment 22* in the bombing area, barely a half dozen would see combat that day, in various states of disrepair, and 28 of their number were smashed beyond retrieval. The staff of the Tiger *Abteilung* quartered in the Emiéville château survived only by huddling in the stairwell of its sturdy tower as the rest of the building crumbled.

On the north-west side of Emiéville is a large private estate, containing within its high walls a trim château and gardens, a stud farm with extensive stabling, and alternating gardens, lawns, racetrack, orchards, and woods, through which meanders a deeply-banked stream. In 2003 the Manneville *'haras'* is owned by the Prime Minister of Lebanon (who rarely visits, preferring his residences in warmer climes). In July 1944, the estate was occupied by *3. Kompanie, 503. s.Pz.Abt.* whose young *Leutnant* Freiherr von Rosen was in temporary command of the company's twelve combat-ready Tiger I tanks. Von Rosen and his men were unhappy with their position, only three miles from the front line:

> We were in a state of permanent readiness. In my opinion, for this task the battalion was located much too far forward.[7]

The Tiger men were more accustomed to being held well behind the lines until an enemy breakthrough threatened, at which point they would be called forward to stabilize the situation.

The Manneville *haras* was on the fringe of the RAF bomb zone. Only isolated sticks of bombs fell across its buildings. Most seriously hit was the eleven-acre wood under whose trees sheltered most of von Rosen's Tiger tanks. Operation Research Section later estimated that 145 heavy bombs fell in and around this area, displacing 40,000 tons of earth and debris.[8] Sheltering under his own tank, Tiger 311, von Rosen lost consciousness.

Twenty-five metres away, *Unteroffizier* Westerhausen's Tiger took a direct hit and blew up; nothing was found of its crew. *Oberfeldwebel* Sachs' Tiger 313 was overturned by the blast of a near miss: *'the fifty eight ton tank was tossed aside like a playing card.'* At last the ordeal ended. An uncanny silence followed, deepened for many by temporary deafness. Von Rosen quickly recovered his senses and took stock. The entire first *Zug* (troop, tanks numbered 311 to 314) was out of action. All the surviving tanks were covered in debris, a deep layer of earth clogging apertures, grilles, and air intakes. Fifteen men had been killed by the bombs. Several of the dead were from the company maintenance section, whose trucks had been blasted to pieces; two of the team disappeared underneath the overturned Tiger. Two men had committed suicide and a third ended in a mental hospital under observation.

With no radios functioning, von Rosen set off on foot to seek orders. At *Abteilung* headquarters, he found the battalion commander, *Hauptmann* Fromme and his staff,

> ...*packed tight together in the narrow winding staircase in the turret of the building.*[9]

Leutnant **Freiherr von Rosen.**

On his return, around 10.00 hours, immediate repairs were well under way. (When the hatch of *313* was forced open, three of its five-man crew were found to have survived.) Six of the Tigers were, if not strictly operational, at least able to move, and it was hoped to get a further two into running order. With no contact between higher-level units, or even between battalion headquarters and its 1 and 2 companies, von Rosen's orders were imprecise: simply to lead his company around the south side of the estate, to guard against any British breakthrough in the direction of Emiéville. The Tiger tanks sputtered and wheezed their way out of the *'haras'*, two of their number falling by the wayside as their engines overheated and caught fire.

Von Rosen found that:

> *My first adopted position, that complied with orders for obstructing a British breakthrough towards Emiéville, was on the southern edge of the haras of Manneville. Since the view and field of fire from this position were limited,*

138

and I heard the noise of battle and engines driving past le Prieuré [due west, recently vacated by Becker's 5. Batterie], I ordered a change of position westwards in the direction of le Prieuré.

The Chateau in the south western corner of the Manneville *'haras'*.

The time was now approaching 11.00 hours. As the Tiger tanks cautiously advanced, a number of 23/Hussars Shermans suddenly appeared directly ahead. All stopped. The Tiger guns fired.

> It was only then that it became clearly evident what hitherto unseen damage the tanks had received during the carpet bombing... all of the tanks' guns were completely out of alignment with their sights. We needed three rounds now where only one would have been adequate before.[10]

Two Shermans were hit; both were destroyed, one with its turret torn clean off by the impact of the heavy 8.8cm shell.

Recommencing their advance, the company reached the small patch of woods due east of le Prieuré. Von Rosen cautiously turned left to skirt the

The avenue of trees today

One of von Rosen's Tigers in the grounds of the Château.

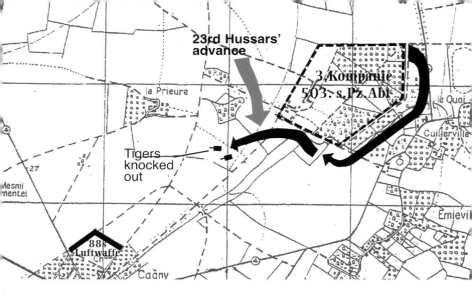

wood, keeping it between his small force and the massed British tanks whose roar he could hear to the west. Suddenly, with two great detonations, *Feldwebel* Schönrock's Tiger went up in flames. Its frontal armour had been cleanly penetrated. This was unprecedented. The *Abteilung* had lost Tiger tanks in Russia to mechanical breakdown, or to flank shots damaging engines or running gear. But no known British weapon could knock out a Tiger through its front armour. Moments later, *Feldwebel* Müller's tank was hit and burning. Apparently facing some new weapon, von Rosen made a rapid decision:

> I broke off the move as I could not pinpoint the source of the fire and did not want to suffer any further total losses.

The counter-attack could have threatened the whole left flank of the British advance. Though enormously outnumbered, with unreliable engines and maladjusted gunsights, a half-dozen Tiger tanks a mile further west, parked across the British armoured corridor, could have brought the day's proceedings to a crashing halt, or at least forced a lengthy delay. While Becker's batteries were a potent striking force they were also vulnerable and depended on their mobility to survive. While the *Luftwaffe* guns in Cagny could force the advancing British to detour westwards, their role was entirely defensive. And, as it transpired years later, it was these same *Luftwaffe* 8.8cm guns which, manned by antiaircraft gunners scanning the horizon for any new target, had stopped von Rosen's attack dead at just

140

A 2.Kompanie Tiger immobilized in the 'haras' grounds during the afternoon.

The fate of one of the Cagny Flak detachment: abandoned before it could be towed away.

over one kilometre range. Ironically, as the survivors of von Rosen's company limped back to Manneville carrying the wounded survivors of their lost tanks, morale having suffered a massive blow, the word went around Guards Armoured Division that Cagny was supported by Tiger tanks as well as emplaced guns. 'Pip' Roberts' warnings were heeded. There would be no haste to take Cagny.

References

1. *Panzer Commander*, Hans von Luck, 1989, ISBN 0-440-20802-5, p 192.
2. From von Luck, interview at Staff College, Camberley, 1979. In other accounts, von Rosen says 'twenty or thirty': his higher estimate was the more accurate.
3. von Luck, interview at Staff College, Camberley, 1979.
4. *21. Panzer-Division,* Jean-Cluade Perrigault, 2002, ISBN 2-84048-157-X, Becker's Monsters, James Barker, IWM Review no. 10, p 26-39.
5. von Luck, p 197.
6. Gooderson, JSS article, p 392.
7. von Rosen, interview at Staff College, Camberley, 1979.
8. Gooderson p 144 & JSS article p 383.
9. Rubbel, p 242.
10. Rubbel p 241.

CHAPTER ELEVEN

TUESDAY, 18 JULY: AFTERNOON

3rd Tanks Onto the Bourguébus Ridge

On the afternoon of 18 July, 3/RTR fought a battle virtually cut off from the rest of VIII Corps by the railway embankment running north-south. As Bill Close's squadron led the way west away from the railway, the entire regimental group made its way under the railway embankment, exchanging the tumult of battle east of the embankment for the light and tranquillity of sunlit cornfields. The leading tanks kept their distance from the ridge as they passed a narrow-gauge rail line serving the industrial area of Cormelles (nowadays a much larger industrial estate). Stopping under cover of a convenient hedgerow, the tank crews squinting into the sun had a *'jolly good look around'*, but still there was no sign of movement on the high ground to the south. Determined as ever to maintain the momentum of the regimental group, Colonel Silvertop at his headquarters, alongside the railway embankment, ordered a reconnaissance of Hubert-Folie.

Twenty year old Lieutenant David Stileman was a platoon commander of 3/RTR's accompanying G Company, 8/Rifle Brigade. His platoon had stopped between the railway and Hubert-Folie when Silvertop made his decision:

At this juncture, it so happened that my platoon headquarters half-track vehicle was some three yards distant from the gallant colonel, and fixing me with those steely eyes, he beckoned me over and said, "Boy, we must find out if Hubert-Folie is occupied".

"Jolly good idea, Sir," I said or something equally fatuous. "How do you propose to do it?"

"You're going to do it," came the reply. And as I swallowed the ever-reassuring Noel Bell [G Company commander] *appeared at my elbow. The plan, like all good plans, was extremely simple. I was temporarily to command a section of the carrier platoon and drive hell-for-leather down the main street of the village. If we failed to appear, the chances were that the village was occupied; but if we emerged unscathed the chances*

143

The sunlit cornfields west of the railway embankment.

*are that the village was not occupied. Now, it so happened that
Noel Bell produced a marvellous air photograph of the village of
Hubert Folie and the surrounding area. Well of course this
meant that I didn't have to fuss around with maps. And also at
this moment [Major] Bill Smythe-Osborne who commanded H
Battery of 13/RHA offered his services. And he decided to put a
heavy artillery concentration down on Hubert Folie as we
approached the village. And the last shell was to be a
phosphorous one, and this [dense white smoke] was the signal
for us to start on our journey down the village. Believe you me,
once we'd started, there was no time for sauntering and within
seconds we appeared at the other end of the village and reported
back to Noel Bell and told him that we had met no resistance and
had seen no sign of the enemy. But how wrong one can be!
Because as we discovered later, the village was groaning with
enemy.[1]*

Noel Bell later supposed:

*The enemy were presumably rather shaken by the sight of
three carriers with all weapons blazing hurtling towards them at
top speed, or else they did not want to disclose their dispositions.[2]*

In fact, apart from infantry outposts sheltering under cover in
the little village itself, the enemy's main strength at that time
was to be found in gun emplacements higher on the crest of the
ridge behind the village. As midday approached, 3/RTR
reorganized, replacing lost troop leaders. Each of the squadrons
had lost over a half a dozen tanks, but still no movement was to

144

be seen by binoculars scanning the ridge, and it was possible to raise some optimism for the afternoon ahead.

Accordingly, the surviving tanks of 3/RTR began their advance from Cormelles due south towards Bras. The objective lay barely a mile away, its roofs masked by trees, while every inch of the tanks' advance was exposed to view from the ridgeline ahead. One tank actually reached the road leading east out of Bras towards Hubert-Folie before the defenders let loose a torrent of Armour Piercing shot. Major Langdon managed to extricate himself and his crew before the ammunition went up and the tank burst into flame, though his gunner was mortally wounded. As smoke billowed from the stricken Sherman, Buck Kite watched from the following tank:

> Bras is at the top of a slope beside a small wood. We started copping it there and I fired back... before the Sherman on my left brewed up. The crew baled out and came over to my tank carrying the gunner, a Scots lad called Hume who used to play for the battalion football team. I thought, 'My God, Hummer, you'll never keep goal again.' Both legs were hanging on by threads of sinew. They got him on the back of my tank and I handed him morphine as I had other things to do.[3]

The fire appeared to be coming from all directions; it is likely that one of Becker's mobile batteries had moved into positions to the west, around Ifs, covering the right flank of the advance, while the guns dug-in above and behind Hubert-Folie and Bras had a field of vision over the battlefield hindered only by smoke

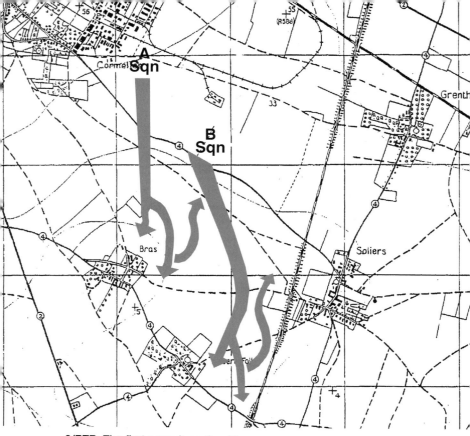

3/RTR: The first assault on the ridge.

from burning tanks. Burning crewmen rolled on the ground to extinguish the flames. Blackened survivors helped each other back through the corn. Some were lifted on to the engine covers of a reversing tank, where the turret might offer some protection. The most fortunate were picked up by 8/RB half-tracks and carriers to be rushed back to an aid post. Both Kite's and the following troops of tanks reversed the way they had come, 'left stick, right stick', zigzagging back down the hill.

As his squadron fell back, Bill Close's own tank was hit with a crash but fortunately did not brew and all baled out unhurt. Close sent the four crewmen back to the cover of the rail embankment (where Silvertop had set up regimental headquarters along with an advanced aid post), and dashed over to take over his sergeant's tank. He was 'rather disconcerted' to find this tank had already been hit and

146

abandoned, so carried on to resume command of the squadron from the troop corporal's tank. Covered by the two surviving Shermans of Buck Kite's troop (one a Firefly) and accompanied by the faithful artillery officer's Stuart, Close organized the survivors of his squadron. But every attempt at further advance was thwarted, and as ammunition began to run low with little prospect of resupply, the tanks regrouped, taking what shelter they could find from vegetation, folds in the ground, or abandoned tanks (whose growing numbers helped by attracting a proportion of the Germans' fire).

B and C Squadrons also took losses in the opening salvoes, and their advance angled away eastwards, away from Bras, skirting Hubert-Folie in their search for a way forward. Two troops of tanks penetrated as far south as the road between Hubert-Folie and Bourguébus, one tank actually reaching the bridge where the railway embankment turned into a cutting passing under that road. Jim Caswell, commanding one of the forward B Squadron tanks,

> ...could only see two Tigers or Panthers in a wood at Bourguébus. Until then everything had gone well.

Then, disaster:

> Several B Squadron tanks were knocked out, some burning. I ordered Barney (Trooper Barnes) to turn left to face the enemy tanks and then reverse... We were now firing at the enemy, but I could tell they were ranging on us. We had reversed about 25 yards and we were hit in the front and the shell killed our gunner, Bill Slater, outright. Stan Duckworth (wireless operator/loader) was seriously wounded in the legs and slumped onto the turret floor.[4]

Though himself wounded in the knee, Jim tried unsuccessfully to open the two forward crew hatches, before giving up and hauling the wounded operator out of the still-reversing tank. Jim carried the operator for an hour to an Advanced Field Dressing Station where he himself collapsed with wounds that ended his Army career. Only twenty years later did Jim learn why the tank had continued moving. Throwing the tank into reverse gear was an instinctive response. (Jim Caswell recalls that when Bingo callers announced the number '88', the audience would roar out 'driver reverse!') Barney the driver had gone a step further by inventing a device to keep the accelerator compressed if he were wounded while reversing. The gadget served its purpose; with its driver dead at the controls the tank continued its unrelenting backwards voyage across the battlefield.

After several attempts to regain the offensive against stiffening opposition, cut off from resupply, 3/RTR began to run low on ammunition. Silvertop bowed to the inevitable and ordered his tanks back to find what cover they could from enemy fire. In addition to fire from distant emplaced guns, increasing numbers of German tanks were appearing through the smoke and dust. Meanwhile, the infantry of the Rifle Brigade had been offering what assistance they could to stricken tank crews. Their carrier platoon suffered heavily, though encouraged by the success of a section commanded by a sergeant which located and neutralized a German artillery observation post on the railway embankment. Noel Bell moved his headquarters behind a hedge which might offer cover from view, if not from fire:

> We seemed to lie behind that hedge for hours, imagining every moment to be our last. I made a great mistake in passing round a bottle of gin, the effect of which lowered everyone's spirits instead of, as I had hoped, bolstering them up.[5]

At length, it became obvious that there was little place for an infantry company in this essentially armoured fight, and Silvertop released Bell's survivors to retire to cover until nightfall.

For 3/RTR, the day ended in leaguer by a quarry alongside the railway embankment. The motor company dug in alongside the tanks and Lieutenant Stileman was again sent forward on a recce – this time to endeavour to cut the Caen-Falaise road during the brief hours of night. But with the surrounding countryside floodlit by still-burning tanks, stealth was impossible. The high hopes of the day had been dashed, and the only compensations were relief at discovering comrades who had survived the action, and the blessing of a few short hours of sleep.

Fifes and Hussars at Four

East of the railway embankment that separated 3/RTR from the rest of VIII Corps, the British advance that had begun with promising lack of resistance had by midday stalled. At the point of furthest penetration, around Four, two squadrons of 2/Fife &

Four: south of the bridge over the railway.

Forfar had proved woefully inadequate to break through a co-
ordinated defensive chain of strongpoints. The small number of
their tanks still in action were preserved largely by the German
gunners' difficulty in distinguishing active Shermans from
those already knocked out, or even friend from enemy, through
the smoke and dust.

29th Brigade HQ was now unable to make contact with any
unit of the Fifes, and it was clear to Brigadier Harvey that they
were in trouble. Help was needed. The 23/Hussars were
ordered forward, but movement was not as easy as it had been
in the morning and their route south was circuitous. By midday,
passage down the 'tank corridor' was becoming more a matter
of running the gauntlet from cover to cover. South of the Caen-
Troarn railway, tanks and other vehicles accumulated behind
the protective screen of the thick hedgerow between the rail line
and le Prieuré. From there, most southbound traffic skirted well
clear of fire from the vicinity of Cagny, routing westward as far
as the road leading to le Mesnil Frémentel, and onward towards
Grentheville, the distant walls and buildings of le Mesnil
serving as cover.

At length, the third tank regiment of 11th Armoured Division arrived in the heart of the battle at around 14.00 hours. Crossing the Caen-Paris railway with very little idea of the situation, and with no word at all from the 2/Fife & Forfar, the Hussars' orders were simply to advance east of the railway embankment to the Bourguébus ridge. The force was entirely composed of tanks, since the attached H Company of 8/Rifle Brigade had been dropped off along the way. The company was assigned the task of securing Grentheville, by-passed by 3/RTR and their own accompanying infantry. With B Squadron leading, the Hussars entered the fray, and soon fell upon the wreckage of the Fifes' own B Squadron, just short of Four.

In a ring of blazing tanks it was impossible to make out any tank still operational. The Fifes' despairing squadron commander welcomed the Hussars with the news that, as far as he could tell, there were only four tanks left in his regiment. (At the end of the day, there remained eighteen, still a huge loss rate.) While this news was being relayed, all four tanks of the Hussar squadron's 1 Troop were hit and in seconds all were blazing. Sergeant Bateman fired back into the murk at an advancing Panther and was seen to score a hit, but moments later died as his turret was cleanly penetrated. Captain Blackman's tank also scored a hit, moments before his tank too exploded in flames.

Like so many tank units that day, the survivors of the Hussars' B Squadron together with the regimental headquarters group engaged reverse gear in search of cover. While Colonel Harding relayed the situation over his wireless to Brigadier Harvey, a pursuing Panther attempted to engage the colonel's tank. The Panther in its turn was stalked by the second-in-command's tank, whose gunner RSM Wass knocked out the German with a critical hit on the big tank's turret ring. It was now 14.25 hours and Colonel Harding was reporting to the Brigadier that the Fifes were too thin on the ground to hold the position, and that consequently he was unable to advance further for fear of leaving an open void to his flank and rear. Far from advancing, the hard-pressed Hussars continued back to shelter under the cover of a hedgerow. And even behind this dubious protection, the position rapidly deteriorated as nearly all the 17-pounder Fireflies had been knocked out, the 75mms were virtually useless, and every few minutes one more Sherman went up in flames.

A Sherman knocked over on its side by a direct hit.

With the Hussars standing their ground as best they could, at 15.00 hours the surviving Fifes pulled back to a map reference some hundreds of yards to the rear to reorganize. They were joined by Captain Hutchinson and his survivors, including Steel Brownlie whose troop was, remarkably, still intact, its only loss a leaderless stray that had attached itself around midday and later was brewed up. Steel Brownlie recognized:

The farm complex of le Poirier, south-east from the railway bridge.

Our lack of casualties was of course due to the good luck of having been hived off to watch the left flank, while the others went on, but in a hectic day we perhaps justified our existence.[6]

The regimental leaguer was a sad affair. At first the Fifes mustered only nine of the sixty or so tanks that had begun the day with such optimism. Later that evening, the number rose to sixteen Shermans, four from C Squadron (including Jack Thorpe's tank which had fought with the Hussars through the afternoon) and twelve from A, whose Major Powell assumed command. Of B Squadron's tanks there was no sign, though two tanks were later brought into the leaguer. All of regimental headquarters' tanks had been brewed, though the second-in-command, Sir John Gilmour, was reported to have survived despite having countless tanks shot from under him and ending the battle riding the regimental bulldozer (actually, a Sherman tank fitted with a dozer blade). Steel Brownlie sums up the mood:

It was the blackest moment in the history of the regiment and not a word was said by anyone except in such phrases as "You know ..... has had it" and so on.

With the Hussars' B Squadron making its desperate stand in front of Four, A Squadron began to arrive to cover their right flank and rear while C Squadron now came up around their left, exploiting a fold in the ground that briefly hid them from enemy fire. Some German tanks emerging from Cagny were fired upon, then the squadron crested the rise.

Bill, my Squadron Leader, [Major W G C Shebbeare] *gave his orders over the wireless in an excited voice, but they were perfectly clear. They were to be his last. The whole Squadron, with the exception of my troop, which was to move forward as his right and flank protection, were to advance towards the village. By this time an incendiary shell had set alight the grass in the field we were in, and a haze of smoke made it difficult to see the other tanks of the Squadron.*[7]

Out of Geoffrey Bishop's field of vision, C Squadron had taken a terrible volley from the defenders of Four, at near point blank range.

As soon as Bill had completed his orders, we started to move slowly forward. Within a few seconds Peter Robson's tank was hit... and went up in smoke. All the crew baled out safely. The rest of the Squadron moved on and I could hear Jock Addison reporting a Panther on the outskirts of the village, which he was trying to engage. This was almost the last coherent message to be heard from the rest of the Squadron.

The regimental history takes up the story:

> *With no time for retaliation, no time to do anything but to take one quick glance at the situation, almost in one minute, all of the tanks of three troops and of Squadron Headquarters were hit, blazing and exploding. Everywhere wounded and burning figures ran or struggled painfully for cover... Major Shebbeare's tank was one of the first to be hit. He was never seen again. Dazed survivors ran to and fro helping the many wounded, beating out flaming clothing with their hands, until the intense heat and violent explosions drove them back to the cover of the railway line... All too clearly, we were not going to "break through" today.[8]*

The only surviving officer of the C Squadron attack, Captain Peter Walter, was getting out of his turret when a passing armour piercing shot injured him in the hand. Nevertheless he assumed command of the squadron, setting about restoring some sort of order. As the increasingly one-sided firefight roared, he supervised the collection of the wounded, the walking wounded helping the more seriously injured back. Then he took command of one of the remaining Fireflies, his gunner claiming a Panther while Walter organized the surviving tanks of the squadron around his position. With an enemy attack forming, and out of contact with any of his supporting artillery, the only channel Walter's operator was able to raise on the radio was the British Broadcasting Company; in

Le Poirier farm complex (the distant Cagny sugar beet factory has replaced the former château).

desperation Walter broadcast one of the most extraordinary requests the BBC has ever received from a listener: 'Hello, this is Peter Walter, I need some artillery fire.'[9] The message was relayed and 13/Royal Horse Artillery played the music with a 25-pounder concentration on the target. Walter was to refuse evacuation for treatment until the end of the following day. For rallying the tanks and putting up a stubborn resistance, he was deservedly to win a DSO. But meanwhile C Squadron was down to six tanks and B faring barely better. Bowing to the inevitable, the remaining tanks of B and C Squadrons together edged back to the Caen-Paris railway line, which offered the relative security of good hull-down positions. It was clear to the Hussars that the question was no longer how to get to the ridge, but how to hang on to the ground already gained.

The situation was becoming desperate. "It seemed to be only a matter of time before the rest of the regiment was written off." For the only time in the European campaign, the Hussars' medical services were unable to keep up with the incoming tide of wounded. Medical Officer Captain Mitchell, his orderlies, and the walking wounded together struggled heroically to overcome the backlog, at one time with seventy badly wounded men awaiting urgent attention:

The Medical Officer had fixed up a temporary Dressing

The railway cutting afforded hull-down positions.

Station in a little white signal box on the railway line and casualties started streaming back from the burnt-out tanks. The chaps were all blackened, their clothes burnt, and most of them had lost their berets. A tank which had survived came roaring back with a lot of wounded lying on the back of it.

The regiment had suffered a *'bloody nose'* and:

A determined enemy advance just at that moment would have been very hard to deal with. But all those Shermans were not blazing in the cornfields for nothing. Many a Panther blazed there too...[10]

Still came orders from Brigade to press forward. From the position by the railway, Bishop reported to Colonel Harding that hull-down defence on the reverse slope of the bank was the best tactic.

Although he did not seem pleased, he said that so long as I understood his first orders that the line was to be held at all costs, I could move to that position.

With the remainder of B and C Squadrons effectively pinned down along the railway, A Squadron became the principal manoeuvre unit of the regiment. About 16.15 hours, with Grentheville still being contested by H Company of 8/RB, A Squadron attempted a long right-hook move, passing between Grentheville and Four then angling left to come at the flank of Four from the west. Attached to the Hussars after losing his squadron of Fife & Forfars, Jack Thorpe recalled:

We go on and begin to climb a high ridge... but we are fired at by German tanks and we find hull down positions.The German tanks come on, advancing down the hill from the crest. Cliff selects one as a target and gives Bert a free hand to fire AP when ready. I see one round hit the German tank, but it is advancing towards us with the thickest part of its armour at the front. The second shot scores a hit on the turret, and yet a third on the side, but all three rounds have ricocheted into the sky as we follow the path of the tracer. Three hits without slowing him down... but now his turret is turning and the long gun is moving round towards us. [The later models of *Panther* tank used by the *Leibstandarte* at GOODWOOD were capable of very fast turret rotation – up to 24 degrees per second – but this depended on the driver keeping high engine revolutions in a high gear ratio; in low gear the turret rotation could be as slow as 4 degrees per second.] *In a few seconds we shall be looking up his muzzle, it's time to back off quickly. Our gun is a bloody toy! We beat a retreat, in reverse, and find cover. We've lost them or they've lost us.*[11]

Meanwhile, F Company of 8/RB advanced to attempt to clear Four. The attempt failed. The motor infantry company fell back to the railway line where the 23/Hussars were grimly hanging on.

Only at sundown did the action slowly die down. As the sun set at the end of the long summer afternoon, the glow of smouldering tanks lit the fields in front of the Hussars' railway position. Leaving behind a thin screen of motor infantry, the tanks fell back a short way to form close leaguer. Not far enough to escape the acrid smell of burnt out vehicles. And before anyone could settle, a final German artillery concentration caught B Squadron's Major Seymour, who was only now at the end of the day seriously wounded. All three sabre squadrons would end the day with new leaders.

Grenadiers and Coldstream Guards

As the last elements of 11th Armoured Division moved off from le Prieuré in the direction of le Mesnil Frémentel, the first regiment of 5th Guards Armoured Brigade debouched from the minefields, crossed the first railway, and took shelter behind the hedgerow. Charged by O'Connor with taking Cagny, Guards Armoured quickly became aware that even approaching the place would be fraught with difficulty. The plan was to advance with two regiments up: 2/(Armoured) Grenadier Guards on the right directed on Cagny while 1/(Armoured) Coldstream Guards secured the left flank, by-passing Cagny to the north. This was not to be.

Once clear of the minefield paths, the Grenadiers were behind schedule, and the Coldstream behind them even more so. The Grenadiers' tanks hurried forward on their own. By 11.00 hours, Lieutenant Heywood's squadron of 2/(Armoured) Grenadier Guards had advanced as far as the hedgerow-lined field on the west side of the walled farm of le Prieuré. (Unbeknown to the Grenadiers, a substantial number of Germans were still occupying the farm, lying low after the departure of the mobile antitank guns.) To Lieutenant Heywood's considerable relief, he was given permission to dwell in this position while number 2 Squadron took the lead.

156

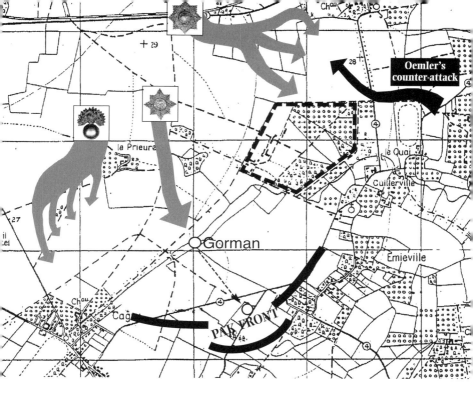

They duly set off over open fields of corn and root vegetables, over which could be discerned the ruins of Cagny and distant columns of oily-black smoke. Antitank fire from the direction of Cagny promptly knocked out two 2 Squadron tanks, and the survivors sought what cover they could find. The regimental commander, Lieutenant Colonel Moore, came forward to get the squadron moving. If Cagny was too strongly held, the tanks should instead attempt to bypass to the north. But attempts to 'feel the way forward' to either flank proved unsuccessful. Soon after Moore returned to his own tank, the number 2 squadron commander's tank was hit and Major Sir Arthur Grant killed.

Advancing with squadrons in line-ahead formation, the Coldstream reached the Caen-Troarn railway, where they prepared to take up their assigned position to the left flank of the Grenadiers. What was going on ahead remained a mystery. All the Coldstream tankers knew was that something was holding up the Grenadiers in front, while behind them vehicles of all types and of all units were crowding the fields. Even with visibility obscured by dust and smoke, German artillery observers could hardly miss such an inviting target. Shells and mortar bombs caused confusion in the rear, while a shell falling amidst the Coldstream headquarters group killed Major Buxton, commanding officer of the accompanying 131 Battery of the Leicestershire Yeomanry. Unlike Germans and Americans, British artillery commanders accompanied the troops their guns were supporting; the system led to enhanced responsiveness but the price was often high. Moving on, the Coldstream's leading 1 Squadron spread out in battle formation while 2 Squadron turned to cover the left flank. *Panther* tanks had been reported in the woods a few hundred yards away to the east, and the crews of 2 Squadron felt exposed in the open fields.

Our tracks were nicely covered in the tall corn, but we were a sitting target to any Panther in the woods.[12]

Counterthrust and Pakfront

Enemy armour was indeed in the woods. Not *Panther* tanks; the only *Panther* in action this afternoon would be those of the *Leibstandarte* descending from the Bourguébus ridge. The movements observed were bigger cats: shortly after midday the counter-attack led by the *Königstiger* of *Oberleutnant* Oemler's *I./s.Pz.Abt. 503* was getting under way and about to break out of the woods on its short-lived advance westward. Having manoeuvred through the bomb-torn lunar landscape of Emiéville and around the wooded estate of the Manneville stud farm, the armoured column emerged from hedgerows along the line of the modern A13 '*Autoroute de Normandie*' and into a very large field.

This forty-acre (fifteen hectares) field was covered in grain, the strains grown in the 1940s standing much taller than modern wheat. The outer sides of the field had been cropped, the hay heaped into stacks, but the harvest had been interrupted by the outbreak of the battle. Even seated in the biggest battle tank in the world, drivers had difficulty seeing where they were going. First *Oberleutnant* Oemler's command *Königstiger* 100 slipped into a bomb crater from which it could not be extricated. Meanwhile, a 1 Squadron Coldstream Firefly commanded by Lieutenant Malcolm Lock was manoeuvring outside the field, roughly in the area today occupied by the British War Cemetery. From this point, Lock claimed to have stalked and 'nicely brewed-up' a *Panther*. In all probability, his victory was in fact scored against *Leutnant* Schroeder's *Königstiger 111*. The King *Tiger* was penetrated, its lieutenant and crewman *Gefreiter* Gükl killed. Moments later, *Königstiger 101* was likewise destroyed.[13] Precise details of this action are hard to verify. Apart from Lock's claim, British sources are strangely silent about the turning of the *Königstiger*-led counter-attack. Some sources confuse the location of the action, even claiming that the armoured column reached as far as Démouville. It most certainly did not. To do so would have entailed passing through 5th Guards Armoured Brigade, which would hardly have gone unnoticed! And such a penetration, astride the narrow British armoured corridor, would quite likely have turned the battle into a British disaster, leaving 29th Armoured Brigade isolated and severed from its supply and support. Of the actual outcome there is no doubt. The counter-attack was broken by a devastating torrent of fire. With it was broken the Tiger crews' self belief and sense of invulnerability. In the smoke and confusion the surviving *Königstiger* and their accompanying *Panzer IV* pulled back.

This was by no means the end of 5th Guards Brigade's troubles. While the Tiger companies pulled back to lick their wounds, and prepare to harry the British flanks, other German defences were coming into play. By midday, the narrow British armoured corridor was coming under increasingly heavy fire from the east. Under cover of woods, orchards, and hedgerows, an antitank '*Pakfront*' ran from as far north as Touffreville (largely untouched by the bombing), and south through

No longer invulnerable, King Tiger 111.

Manneville and Emiéville to Frénouville, while isolated guns were in place as far forward as the orchards around Cagny. The infantry's own antitank guns were supplemented by specialized units under command of *LXXXVI Korps* such as *Artillerie-Pak-Abteilung 1053*. Though designated as '*bodenständige*' (that is, static), the unit had been able to find transport to convey sixteen *Pak 40* guns to the general area of Touffreville, each with its sixty 7.5cm rounds (thirty *Sprenggranate 34* [High Explosive] and thirty *Panzergranate 39* [Armour Piercing] in a nearby trench, when possible actually under the breech of the gun, between its split trails). As the surviving crews recovered from the shock of the bombing, they manned their pieces, repaired camouflage, cleaned off the debris, and prepared to engage. Waiting until Sherman tanks were a mere 300 metres distant, a first-time hit was almost a certainty, and barring a 'dud' shell, a hit anywhere on the Sherman meant a near certain kill. Certainly, any crew that survived such a hit would be quick to bale out, regardless of standing orders to await the command.

As the afternoon wore on, the *Pakfront* was to be further stiffened by the arrival of *Artillerie-Pak-Abteilung 1039,* also under command of *LXXXVI Korps*, with its twenty-seven purpose built *Pak 43,* in range and killing power largely the most potent antitank gun the German artillery possessed. Designed to kill the heaviest Russian tanks, the enhanced armour penetration capability of the 8.8cm round was arguably

The field where Oeler's counter-attack came to grief, viewed from the south corner of the War Cemetery.

N◄———————

Abandoned Pak 40 at Sannerville.

redundant when opposing Shermans and Cromwells. The main benefit as compared to the 7.5cm Armour Piercing round was the greater weight of explosive filler, designed to detonate after the target's armour was penetrated, reducing the chances of crew survival. In theory, the guns' range allowed them to 'stand off' at arm's length from attacking tanks, though again this advantage was of less benefit on the battleground between Cagny and Emiéville, where there were no commanding heights and the field of vision was limited by grain and trees, dust and smoke. In practice, on the afternoon of 18 July, the superior performance of these awesome weapons was largely offset by their weight and bulk, and the need to get them into forward positions quickly. Ideally such guns would be painstakingly dug in and camouflaged, a process which could take upwards of a full day. On 18 July, many of the guns engaged the enemy before they could even be separated from their carriage of two sets of bogie wheels; in this state the gun's traverse was limited to thirty degrees either side and – crucially – it offered a larger target. After the action, the commander of *Art.-Pak.-Abt. 1039*, *Hauptmann* Witzel, was commended for his considered and brave leadership (*'umsichtigen und tapferen Führung'*) which achieved the destruction of thirty five tanks. The price paid for this included Witzel's own life and the loss of at least a dozen of his guns.

Pak 43 of 1039.Abt. hastily unlimbered north of Cagny, destroyed by a direct hit.

Coldstream and Irish Guards

By the early afternoon, 5th Guards Brigade Headquarters was established near le Prieuré. Amid the confusion typical of the day, troops of Coldstream tanks were advancing cautiously towards the farm, not realizing it was in friendly hands. Meanwhile a tank attached to the HQ saw a movement in the place and put a few canon shells into the farm buildings. To the amazement of the HQ staff a hundred Germans gave themselves up. 'If they had chosen to fight, Brigade would have looked very silly.' The advancing Coldstream were ordered in no uncertain terms by the brigadier to get a move on, transferring from the left flank of the attack around to the right, in an attempt to outflank Cagny to the west and south while the third tank regiment of the brigade, 2/Armoured Irish Guards took their place in the fight. The Coldstream duly set off, passing le Prieuré on their left and setting a course across cornfields for Cagny. No one knew what to expect. Was Cagny in friendly or enemy hands? Then the ruins of the place came into view, and the Coldstream,

> *...saw a sight that rather shook us all... the horizon was covered with burning Shermans. I could count nearly twenty, a whole squadron, burning in one field alone. More were hidden behind the black smoke of others brewing up, while yet others were still being hit and bursting into flames.*[14]

The Coldstream colonel quickly decided that 'We must not add to this disaster,' and the unit looped more widely around the ruins of Cagny, towards the Caen-Paris railway whose earth banks and hedgerows promised the best available shelter. In this vicinity, along the railway between Cagny and Four, the Coldstream fought to hold their ground for the rest of the afternoon.

Meanwhile, their arrival delayed by traffic jams until the afternoon, the tanks of 2/Armoured Irish Guards were welcomed to the battlefield by the dismal sight of nine Grenadier Guards tanks burning ahead, while from the fields and woods to the left German guns were firing steadily. The order was to advance over the fields north of Cagny; since the place appeared too strongly held to be quickly taken, it could perhaps instead be surrounded. Once past the woods around le Prieuré, the countryside opened up into large, rolling fields intersected by hedgerows of varying density. This was the sort of country the regiment had trained for. The colonel, Lieutenant Colonel Kim Finlay instructed the lead squadron simply to follow the electricity pylons which, helpfully, traversed the fields on a roughly east-west axis. Over the open country, like huntsmen following the pack, the Irish Guards set off.

But before the open fields could be reached, the hunters had first to cross the Ruisseau de Cagny, a small stream running due north out of the devastated village. Itself only a narrow trickle, the rivulet was in places surrounded by patches of flat, boggy ground, and it was in one of these that Lieutenant John Gorman's *Ballyragget* became stuck fast. Ordering his Troop Sergeant Evans to carry on the advance with half the troop including the Firefly, Gorman spent an impatient half hour supervising the freeing of his own Sherman by the troop's number four tank using a steel towrope. Then, pressing forward

with all possible speed to catch up with his own tanks, Gorman came upon his own 2 Squadron, halted around its commander Tony 'Dipper' Dorman:

> *'Dipper' was on his feet, evidently wounded, but gesticulating wildly forward. Since the whole strategy of our leftwards attack on Cagny had been to take it by the speed and dash which we had learned on Salisbury Plain and the Yorkshire Wolds, I took it that Dipper was urging us on and we hared up a cornfield, towards a hedge at the top of the rise.*[15]

In fact, the leading troops of the squadron had been held up by the intensity of the antitank fire to their front. Amid the dust and uncertainty of the battle, Gorman's daring advance appeared to have stolen a march on the enemy. Then, cresting the gentle slope and rounding the end of a hedgerow, Gorman was appalled to see just three hundred yards ahead the great bulk of a *Königstiger*.

Belonging to *1. Kompanie* of the *503.s.Pz.Abt.*, the great tank had become separated from its unit in the confusion of the battle. Its commander was an inexperienced sergeant, *Feldwebel* Gerber, who had only recently been attached to the *Abteilung* to gain combat experience and (he hoped!) the possibility of a decoration. As the *Kompanie* withdrew from its abortive attack, manoeuvring around Manneville towards Frénouville, his *Königstiger* number 112 lost contact with his company and,

> *...the inexperienced commander lost his nerve and drove through the area in a fairly disoriented manner.*[16]

Engaged by more than one British tank, the gunner Hans-Joachim Thaysen returned fire, but the commander panicked and ordered the driver, Horst Becher, to reverse, taking the Tiger through a hedge.

Gorman had previously discussed with *Ballyraggett's* driver Lance Corporal Baron what they might do if they ever came across a Tiger tank. Agreeing that the 75mm gun was unlikely to be of much use in such a situation they had speculated as to whether the naval tactic of ramming might be appropriate. Now, Gorman ordered gunner Albert Scholes to 'Traverse left – on – fire!' The High Explosive round bounced off the *Königstiger* and rocketed up into the air. Ordered to keep firing, Scholes's hollow voice replied 'Gun jammed, Sir.' Gorman hesitated a moment, found that his training did not cover the situation, then remembering the discussions with Baron, he gave the order, 'Driver, ram!' Baron accelerated *Ballyraggett* towards the behemoth, then crashed into its left rear.

Already disoriented, the German commander was further confused by the HE shell glancing off his turret, then the almighty impact of thirty tons of Sherman tank. A moment later, the *Königstiger* was penetrated by an Armour Piercing round entering the left side between the running gear and the track, and taking the gunner's seat out from under him. (Thaysen maintains that this was a 7.5cm German round from a *Pak 40*, presumably aimed at *Ballyraggett*; this is not at all unlikely, as there were German antitank guns emplaced nearby.) Already displeased with their commander's performance, the crew were quick to follow him as he abandoned the stricken *Panzer*. Gorman's crew likewise abandoned the immobilized *Ballyraggett*, and there were awkward moments as two crews faced off. Gunner Thaysen recalls his encounter with co-driver Guardsman Agnew:

> *For a moment we looked at each other in a daze. Then a rush of heroism awoke in both of us. Each grabbed for the place where he'd usually find his pistol. Heroism failed for a lack of lethal materials... We eyed each other and each tried to convince the other, with hands and feet, that the other was his prisoner. Since it turned out that each of us had opposite opinions about that, both of us shrugged our shoulders, grinned at each other, and bolted for our own sides.*

Meanwhile, Gorman led the other three crewmen back to the shelter of Sergeant Pat Harbinson's tank, which had followed their advance, but the Sherman was destroyed by enemy fire before they reached it. Gorman pressed on across fields until he came upon a Firefly whose commander, Sergeant Workman, had been decapitated. The sergeant's body was draped over the breech of the gun and to either side the gunner and operator were in shock. Gorman took charge, the gory mess was wiped

"'Driver, ram!' Baron accelerated *Ballyraggett* towards the behemoth, then crashed into its left rear."

The King Tiger was penetrated by a round entering over its left track; a later round penetrated the turret of Gorman's (abandoned) Sherman.

off gunsights and periscopes, and the Firefly advanced to the disabled *Königstiger* where further rounds were put into the German to ensure its destruction. By this time, Harbinson's Sherman was well ablaze, and Gorman transported the mortally wounded sergeant and his two surviving crew back to the regimental aid post.

Gorman won the Military Cross for his exploit, which proved a tonic to the regiment. But the Irish Guards' cavalry charge had not lived up to their own expectations. Guards Armoured Division would take time to learn the necessity of co-operation between tanks and infantry.

The End of the First Day

As afternoon turned to evening, it was clear that British gains were to fall far short of expectations. West of the railway embankment, 3/RTR were hanging on by the skin of their teeth, and to its east the surviving Hussars had likewise abandoned thoughts of progressing south of the Caen-Paris railway. 'Pip' Roberts' infantry brigade had successfully cleared the villages behind the armoured advance, but theirs was a separate battle, and by the time they were relieved by elements of 51st Highland Division there was little more they could do.

On the eastern side of the battle, the Guards' infantry brigade was in difficulty. In the forefront of the brigade, 3/Irish Guards had a frustrating afternoon sitting in traffic jams, feeling vulnerable in their unarmoured trucks. Ordered to dig in west of Cagny, they had just completed the job when they were moved off again. First Number 2 Company marched off into the deepening gloom, not to be seen until the following day, then Number 1 followed and could not be retrieved. Summoning his remaining company commanders, Colonel Vandeleur began to brief them for an assault on Cagny. Sadly, he had just uttered the words, *'Never was there more confusion at the start of an operation...'* when the tank on which he had propped his map unexpectedly drove off.

The cautious advance of Guards Armoured towards Cagny finally resulted in 2/Grenadiers tanks and King's Company, 1/(Motor) Grenadier Guards infantry entering the ruins around 18.00 hours. By the time Vandeleur's Irish Guards followed and Cagny was at length reported cleared, night was approaching and the infantry contented themselves with digging-in among the tombstones of Cagny cemetery. A handful of defenders were taken along with the wrecks of the *Luftwaffe* antiaircraft guns, which had lingered too long to escape. But behind Cagny, and northward past Emiéville, the Guards had not broken the *Pakfront*. Up and down the German line, Guards tanks were stopped by guns and lacked the infantry to clear a way forward. As night fell, behind the protective screen, von Luck's *Kampfgruppe* was relieved by leading elements of the *Hitlerjugend*. (Ironically, in von Kluge's possession at that time were sealed orders to be opened in the event of a successful coup against Hitler; should the forces in the west capitulate to the Allies, *21. Panzerdivision* was to be allocated the unwelcome task of disarming *12. SS-Panzerdivision*, the loyal Hitler Youth.)[17]

7th Armoured Division had made little impact on the battle. Delays imposed by traffic jams were compounded by lack of enthusiasm. Divisional commander Major General Erskine disapproved of the whole plan and was quite content for his division to be last to engage in what he felt a gross misuse of armour. Around midday, 'Pip' Roberts encountered Brigadier ('Looney') Hinde, making a forward reconnaissance in advance of the Desert Rats' 22nd Armoured Brigade. *'This is good,'* reflected Roberts, *'We will soon have 7th Armoured Division to take over the area between us and Guards Armoured.'* But it was not to be. Hinde responded, *'There are too many bloody tanks here already; I'm not going to bring my tanks down yet.'* And he departed before Roberts could point out that most of the tanks on view were knocked out. In the end, the leading squadron of 5/Royal Tank Regiment reached the Caen-Paris railway about 17.30 hours. By 18.00 a mistaken report located them in Soliers; in fact they spent the last hours of daylight holding ground just south of Grentheville.

On the flanks of GOODWOOD, Canadian 2nd Corps had fought their own intense and bloody battles for the southern outskirts of Caen. Colombelles was at last cleared and fighting continued through the night for a foothold in Vaucelles. By

1/Welsh Guards advancing on Cagny. The company commander, pointing, is indistinguishable from his men.

morning the German defenders had given up and retired to the Bourguébus ridge. To the west, British 1st Corps had succeeded in breaking out of the long-established 'Airborne perimeter' and were moving through the wooded hills of Bavent. The outskirts of Troarn were reached, but resistance remained bitter. Both these battles are stories in their own right.

If the greatest failure of the first day was the Allies' inability to punch their armoured corridor deeper into the German lines, then perhaps the greatest success was the preservation of that narrow corridor from being outflanked or penetrated. Before the battle, Dempsey had declared himself *'prepared to lose two or three hundred tanks'*, which was just as well since 11th Armoured had already lost 126 in a single day's combat. Crucially, the depleted tank regiments, leaguered for the short night at the point of the breakthrough, remained in touch with their supply lines. Not all were supplied: neither the 23/Hussars nor the few surviving Fife & Forfar tanks received ammunition until next day, and some of the infantry units' Q-trucks failed – most unusually – to make their way forward with an evening meal (one 4/KSLI company was fortunate that their commander had the foresight to equip his jeep with a hundred-tin crate of corned beef for just such an event). Wounded were evacuated, and replacement crews came forward. Engineers completed new crossings over the Orne River and the Caen Canal. And the Forward Delivery Squadrons brought up the new tanks to reorganization areas where gathered surprisingly large number of crews who had survived the loss of their mounts.

Remaining in possession of much of the battlefield also enabled British tank units to recover disabled tanks. While the medics tended the wounded, the R.E.M.E. Light Aid Detachments' recovery vehicles and mechanics worked heroically to recover abandoned tanks before German booby-trap teams could reach them, and (where possible) repaired potential runners. They were not alone. Squadrons sent forward more-or-less willing 'volunteers' to seek and return abandoned tanks in running order. Jack Thorpe was carried forward into the darkness riding on the engine covers of his major's tank before being dropped off to seek a lost Sherman:

> I reach it and carefully assess it. All quiet, both tracks are on it. I decide it is deserted. Then alongside it I see, less than fifteen feet away, a burning-out Panther tank, still glowing red hot, with blue and green copper flames still licking up out of its turret.[18]

On his return to the leaguer with an intact Sherman, Thorpe's fellow crewmen were less than impressed by his failure to loot its ration store for any tins of pears. On 3/RTR's front, a similarly charged 'volunteer' venturing forth into the night could clearly hear Jim Caswell's tank in the distance, its tracks still thrashing the ground where it had apparently reversed into some solid obstacle.

If German logistics did not permit generous levels of resupply, at least replacement units were available. This came at a price. By sucking two *SS-Panzer* divisions into the action, the GOODWOOD assault not only deprived the German high command of the flexibility to redeploy strategically important units, but additionally removed any chance of further resting and re-fitting them for future battles. The infantry units of *1.SS-Panzerdivision* moving up onto Bourguébus ridge during the night of 18-19 July were far from fresh, and full of dread of a repetition of the aerial bombardment of the previous morning.

In fact, the next air assault was that most rare event: a co-ordinated *Luftwaffe* bombing raid. Around 23.30 hours, a number of German aircraft attacked the area of the vital bridges. None of the bridges was damaged, but such was the concentration of traffic at the bottleneck that it was almost impossible for bombs to avoid hitting someone. Main HQ of 11th Armoured Division was hit and suffered losses.

Many survivors of the day's fighting were caught in the rear

Clearing the ruins of Démonville.

echelon reorganization areas. The Hussars lost fitters as well as tank crewmen. The Fife & Forfar who had lost sixty-six officers and men in the day's fighting suffered a further forty-nine casualties in the bombing, another ten tank crews lost.[19]

References

1. Stileman, interview at Staff College, Camberley, 1979.
2. Bell, p 28.
3. Moore, p 147.
4. Caswell diary.
5. Bell, p 28.
6. Steel Brownlie diary.
7. *The Battle*, Geoffrey Bishop, undated, p 45-46.
8. Bishop, 23/Hussars, p 76.
9. Sweet, p 86.
10. Bishop, 23/Hussars, p 76.
11. Thorpe diary.
12. *Armoured Guardsman*, Robert Boscawen, 2001, ISBN 0 85052 748 1, p 31.
13. *45 Tiger en Normandie,* Didier Lodieu, 2002, ISBN 2-84673-015-6, p 85-85; see also Rosse & Hill, p 41; Boscawen p 31.
14. Boscawen, p 33.
15. *The Times of My Life*, Sir John Gorman, 2002, ISBN 0 0 85052 906 9, p 38.
16. Personal correspondence with Richard Freiherr von Rosen. This story has been told with many variations. The version presented here is the author's assessment based on all available evidence.
17. Wilmot, p 418.
18. Thorpe diary.
19. Sellar, p 170-171.

The railway embankment divided the battlefield.

Bourguébus

N

CHAPTER TWELVE

WEDNESDAY, 19 JULY:
ONCE MORE UNTO THE BREACH

Morning

Despite losing over half its tanks the previous day, 11th Armoured Division remained in the front line. There was to be no thought of abandoning the offensive. Like a football team battling for an important trophy but several goals down at half time, VIII Corps had to carry on. But the nature of the battle had changed entirely. Though German eyes scanned the northern horizon with grave apprehension, there was to be no return of the strategic bombing force. Nor was there any hope left of 'breakthrough'. From now on, the battle would be fought for more limited objectives.

'Pip' Roberts' first action of the day was to inform 7th Armoured Division that his own 11th would require the first few hours of daylight for his armoured brigade to reorganize. It remains a tribute to the resilience of 29th Armoured Brigade that any of its units were capable of contemplating further action so soon. The Fifes had enough surviving and replacement tanks to form two squadrons, A and C, each with eleven tanks, and a regimental headquarters of just two Shermans. 3/RTR managed to field three squadrons, with ten tanks each. Though the Hussars had lost fewer tanks, their officer losses were severe and they were held in reserve all day. Freed of supporting the infantry brigade, the 2/Northants Yeomanry were available to Brigadier Harvey, and as early as 06.00 hours their C Squadron was reconnoitring forward, due south towards Bourguébus, and later to a position south-east of Cormelles. Also during the morning the companies of 8/Rifle Brigade were brought together into a single formation, under command of their Colonel, Tony Hunter. And not far behind the armour, the division's infantry brigade around le Mesnil Frémentel now reverted to divisional control.

About 10.30 hours, 'Pip' Roberts received his orders for the day. He was to resume the push south, specifically to take and hold Bras, and so dominate the Caen-Falaise road. He was achieve this without the previous day's heavy bombing, with comparatively little artillery support, and of course with a division much-depleted in the preceding twenty-four hours. But in one crucial respect, Roberts and his fellow division commanders had an advantage denied them the previous day. They were free to plan their own battles. The micro-management of 18 June by VIII Corps had reached ridiculous extremes. At one point in the battle O'Connor came forward to see for himself what was holding things up. He was observed riding a Sherman belonging to the commander of a Guards tank regiment. With the Corps Commander, on the back of the tank, perched the commanders of 5th Guards Armoured Brigade and Guards Armoured Division. In other words: regimental, brigade, division, and corps commanders were all exposed together on the same vehicle; all limiting their view of the battle to the perspective of front-line soldiers; and *'all urgently ordering one another on in descending orders of seniority.'*[1] A trooper of the Second Household Cavalry watching from his armoured car commented,

> *Well, I thought that when I had the Colonel and two other bastards giving advice on the back of my Daimler at Linney Head it was bad enough, but three Generals is bloody murder!*

On 19 July things were different. The three divisional commanders, Roberts, Erskine, and Adair, met late in the

On 19 July the ridge remained to be taken.

Hubert Folie

morning at 'Pip' Roberts' Tac HQ to co-ordinate their plans for the day; and at 12.00 hours, O'Connor arrived and approved the plans they presented.

Bras

11th Armoured was to move at 16.00 hours to take Bras. Once this foothold on the ridge was established, the adjacent village of Hubert-Folie would be attempted. Meanwhile, 7th Armoured Division would take Soliers and Bourguébus, and the Guards secure the le Poirier farm and press on towards Frénouville. 'Pip' Roberts' plan now assigned the proper roles to the different parts of his division. Tanks would lead, accompanied by appropriate quantities of armoured infantry to seize the villages, and 'leg' infantry would come forward to secure and hold them against the inevitable counter-attack. All in all, a sequence of events very different from the preceding day.

The initial assault on Bras was to be led by the 2/Northants' Cromwell tanks, closely supported by 8/RB. 'Pip' Roberts personally warned the Northants' commander to beware of German guns in Ifs, away to the west of the Caen-Falaise road, which had accounted for some of the 3/RTR tanks the previous day. It was agreed that the attack should go in from the north-east of Bras. The regiment set off, C Squadron on the right; A Squadron left; B Squadron in reserve. However, reconnoitring from the Caen-Paris railway line, it was not easy to spot the precise position of Bras. Even today, with the little village larger

Bras   Ifs

N

than in 1944, most of the buildings are screened by trees, and the place lacks a distinctive church tower such as marks the centre of Hubert-Folie. The Northants accidentally wandered west as far as the Caen-Falaise road. It was too far. Five tanks were quickly lost to long range antitank fire and to *Panzerfaust*-armed grenadiers in the corn. The unit became temporarily disordered.

The plan was flexible. Seeing what had happened, the commander of 3/RTR requested that his regiment take the lead, and this Roscoe Harvey promptly agreed. While 2/NY reorganized, 3/RTR would lead the way up the hill to Bras. Though no heavy artillery was to be available and only a single medium regiment on call to suppress the emplaced defenders, the divisional 25-pounder regiments were today closely integrated. Both field regiments, the Sextons of 13/Royal Horse Artillery and the newly-arrived towed guns of the Ayrshire Yeomanry, put down a smoke barrage on the ridge behind Bras, effectively isolating the coming battle from outside interference. The contest would be simply an élite *Panzergrenadier* battalion, established in a hilltop village, versus half-strength English tank and motor infantry regiments advancing over open ground.

At 16.25 hours, tanks charged through the cornfields closely accompanied by two companies of motor infantry, F Company left and H Company right:

> *The motor companies were in their half-tracks until the village was reached and the carriers, thrashing through the corn like destroyers, rounded up many prisoners on the way in. The leading companies reached the village just behind the 3rd Royal Tanks. They jumped out of their vehicles and set about clearing the houses. There was much opposition. Germans with panzerfausts appeared everywhere; several anti-tank guns opened up.*[2]

Individual tanks moved just inside the village, stone walls protecting their flanks while they shot the infantry onto the defenders. The motor infantry plunged into the buildings, catching Germans as they emerged from their shelters. Carried on by the momentum of the attack, by 17.20 hours one F Company platoon led by Philip Sedgwick had fought its way to the far side of the village. Now the open country played against the defenders, as their avenue of retreat was swept by fire. While the three remaining tanks of Bill Close's A Squadron,

> *...had an excellent shoot at some fleeing Germans... B and C*

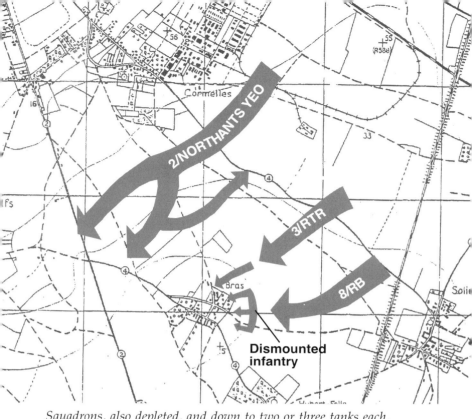

Dismounted infantry

Squadrons, also depleted, and down to two or three tanks each, entered the village at the same time. We were able to knock down the walls of houses from where cowering Germans emerged with their hands raised. Antitank guns were knocked out at point blank range.[3]

By 17.40 hours the village was effectively clear. The entire 3 *Bataillon* of *1.S-Panzergrenadier-Regiment* had been eliminated.

VIII Corps' history records:

This little action is not only of text-book perfection, but the prize thereby won was of the utmost importance to the Corps.[4]

After the disappointments of the previous day, securing a lodgement on the Bourguébus ridge was indeed a welcome development. But in truth, this particular text book had not yet been written. Only in the aftermath of Operation GOODWOOD, on 25 July, did Brigadier Harvey put his signature to a secret document detailing lessons learned including the details of tank and motor infantry co-operation in reducing a village strongpoint.

Hubert-Folie

Now came the turn of Hubert-Folie. Even before 8/Rifle Brigade's H and F Companies had handed over Bras to the infantry of 3/Monmouths, E (Support) and G Companies were preparing for the attack on Hubert-Folie, to be led by the tanks of 2/Northants Yeomanry, who were ordered forward at 18.10 hours. There followed a pause following a report that elements of 7th Armoured Division's 22nd Armoured Brigade were already in the village. Someone had mis-read a map. But the Northants attack had been thrown into some confusion, and by 18.30 they were reported to be taking heavy losses, reduced to a single squadron, and unable to continue forward. The regimental history records that:

Two complete troops returned on their feet after losing their tanks.[5]

At 18.40, it was decided that the Fifes should do the job.

The Fifes' tanks moved up to a position north-east of Hubert-Folie, mortared and shelled all the way. At 20.00 hours they attacked: C Squadron leading, followed by A. Meanwhile, G Company of 8/RB advanced from the direction of Bras. With 10 and 11 Platoon up and 12 Platoon in support, the first infantry reached Hubert-Folie at 20.35. G Company commander Noel Bell recalled:

The village had been previously shelled and the tanks were pumping stuff into it too. [Both the accompanying Fifes and also the survivors of 3/RTR gathered around Bras.] *As the motor platoons moved in I called over the air for the tanks to stop firing but one went on firing and nothing could be done to stop it. It later transpired that this was a tank knocked out the day before and a German was manning its machine gun. The carriers who were acting as flank protection ahead of the motor platoons came under fire from this machine gun, and Cpl. Isard, a very old and popular member of the Company, was killed. We later had the satisfaction of this German "brewed up" in no uncertain manner at very close range.*[6]

E Company followed G into Hubert-Folie, Rifleman Roland Jefferson using his 'sword' (as the Rifles called their bayonet) for the first and only time:

A German, taller and thicker than I, was backing slowly round the corner towards me... I lunged and the sword went into his back.[7]

The German was more terrified than wounded, readily surrendering while Jefferson carefully cleaned the blade lest he be captured with German blood still on his weapon. By 21.15 hours, Hubert-Folie had been taken.

Even within a division as close-knit as 11th Armoured, regimental pride prevented acknowledgement of fellow regiments' achievements. Noel Bell concluded simply that *'a battalion of our infantry brigade arrived on the scene.'* In fact, the advance of 4/King's Shropshire Light Infantry up three hundred yards of open slopes from the railway to Hubert-Folie was a classic infantry action. Lieutenant Mike Sayer was a C Company platoon commander:

> *The advance on Hubert-Folie was an infantryman's nightmare. There we were in a huge open field of corn dominated by high ground ahead and a railway embankment on the* [left] *flank, from which the enemy machine gunners and artillery FOOs had us in full view. At first we were encouraged by the sight of a squadron of tanks, in battle formation, ahead of us but to our astonishment and discomfiture it became apparent that they had all been knocked out on the previous day.*[8]

Even before the Rifle Brigade could work through to the eastern side of the village, the 4/KSLI Carrier Platoon was already around that flank and was giving covering fire. Casualties were heavy. The new Colonel Clayton who had joined the battalion the previous night was hit by airburst and evacuated to have thirty-six pieces of 'shrapnel' dug out of his back. In the absence of cover, those who fell in the tall grain were marked by their rifle with bayonet in the ground and helmet on top before their mates rushed onward. By 21.15 hours, 4/KSLI were in Hubert-Folie, and frantically dug-in around the place. Company commander Ned Thornburn *'did not normally dig my own slit-trench'* but now dug frantically in the soft sandy soil as mortar bombs descended:

> *I don't think I have ever been in such a flat spin as I was for the first few minutes at Hubert-Folie. However, by 22.00 hours the company was adequately dug in and prepared for any eventuality.*[9]

Bourguebus and Frenouville

By 04.30 hours on 19 July, the last fighting units of 7th Armoured Division were finally across the Orne bridges. Action resumed in the morning, before the commanders' conference. With Soliers and Four still in enemy hands, the divisional plan for the day was to use Grentheville as a firm base from which to move south, with the intention of assaulting Bourguébus by 17.00 hours, in co-ordination with 11th Armoured's attack on Bras. In the event, a single squadron of 5/RTR reached the outskirts of Bourguébus by 18.40 hours, to be held up by German tank fire from the village itself. By 20.40 hours, 5/RTR was on all sides of the village, but still it held out. The conquest of Four was also was proving troublesome. By nightfall, Bourguébus was still in German hands, and although Soliers and Four were occupied by elements of 7th Armoured, German infiltration was continuing and the forward regiments' positions were by no means secure.

Guards Armoured Division continued to make little progress against the German line north of Cagny (although we now know that the defending units paid a heavy price for their resistance). All this time, British 3rd Infantry Division was grinding southwards on a front stretching from Cuillerville to Troarn, the fight for Troarn especially bitter. At about 17.00 hours, 1/Welsh Guards infantry attacked the farm of le Poirier and captured it, as planned, and from this position Guards Armoured was able to support 7th Armoured's attempts on Four. Some progress was made from Cagny in the direction of Frénouville, and during the evening a renewed attack with air support was planned for first light.

References

1. *The Household Cavalry at War*, Roden Orde, Aldershot 1953, p 72.
2. *The Rifle Brigade*, Major R H W S Hastings, 1950, p 362.
3. Close, p 129.
4. Jackson, p 106.
5. *The 1st and 2nd Northamptonshire Yeomanry*, Major D G Bevan, 1946.
6. Bell, p 29.
7. *Soldiering at the Sharp End,* diary of Roland Jefferson BEM, 1985.
8. *The 4th KSLI in Normandy*, Major 'Ned' Thornburn, 1990, p 77.
9. Thornburn, p 78.

CHAPTER THIRTEEN

THURSDAY, 20 JULY: STORMY WEATHER

Winding Down

During the night of 19 - 20 July, it became clear to VIII Corps that 11th Armoured was, for the time being, a spent force. All momentum from the 18 July break-in was now lost, and there was little point sacrificing the armoured divisions to take villages which might eventually fall to the infantry. The vital gain of 19 July was the crest of the Bourguébus ridge, and at 22.00 hours on 19 July, orders were passed to 3rd Canadian Division to take over the area held by 11th Armoured, including Bras and Hubert-Folie, by 10.00 hours on 20 July. This the Canadians were well placed to do following their successful operations south of Caen on 19 July. The relief of 3/Monmouths was interrupted by a German counter-attack, but by midday Bras was safely in Canadian hands.

The Guards' planned attack on Frénouville went in, with air support, at 05.45 hours. 1/Welsh Guards and 5/Coldstream Guards charged in unopposed to find the place had been evacuated the previous night. In 7th Armoured Division's sector, B Squadron 5/RTR attacked Bourguébus at first light, destroying one German tank and encountering no further opposition. The division gave support to Canadian moves in the direction of Ifs and Verrières.

Suddenly the weather changed. About 16.00 hours there began a violent thunderstorm. Allied aircraft was grounded. Within a short time, entrenchments began to flood and soon all tracks except metalled roads became impassable to wheeled vehicles.

This battle was over. At 10.00 hours on 21 July, VIII Corps ceased to have responsibility for any section of the front, and Operation GOODWOOD was terminated.

Storm in the East and the West

Meanwhile, unbeknown to most on the battlefield, there had been an attempt on the life of the *Führer*. Twice before, Klaus von Stauffenberg had attended the *Führerhauptquartier* carrying a bomb in his briefcase. On the morning of 20 July, he flew to

Rastenburg determined to execute the plan. At 12.42 hours (German time) the bomb destroyed the conference hut and Hitler barely escaped death.

For many in the German army the eventual outcome was suspicion followed by trial, torture, and death. One destined to die was Rommel: now incapacitated, far from the battlefield, and unable to influence events in the field. Von Kluge hesitated to commit himself long enough to learn that the attempted coup had failed, then proceeded to write his own death warrant on 21 July by recording his strategic assessment of GOODWOOD:

> My discussion yesterday with the commanders in the Caen sector has afforded regrettable evidence that, in face of the enemy's complete command of the air, there is no possibility of our finding a strategy which will counterbalance its truly annihilating effect, unless we give up the field of battle.

The material damage inflicted by the GOODWOOD aerial bombardment fell far short of expectations. But its morale impact was huge.

Sadly for the German soldiers in Normandy, the effect of the failed coup was to stifle any further German plans for a local surrender of German forces to the British and American Allies. At the operational level, it became even harder to gain permission to give up ground. The armies stood and bled instead of following a more logical course of staged withdrawal.

For the Allies, this continuing German resistance was infuriating, and much of the fury was directed against Montgomery. The Americans, Eisenhower among them, felt betrayed by the apparent failure of GOODWOOD. Though destined to retain his status among the British as a war hero, Montgomery's image among the Americans, and his personal influence over high strategy, never recovered from the blow.

References

1. *The Household Cavalry at War*, Roden Orde, Aldershot 1953, p 72.
2. *The Rifle Brigade*, Major R H W S Hastings, 1950, p 362.
3. Close, p 129.
4. Jackson, p 106.
5. *The 1st and 2nd Northamptonshire Yeomanry*, Major D G Bevan, 1946.
6. Bell, p 29.
7. *Soldiering at the Sharp End,* diary of Roland Jefferson BEM, 1985.
8. *The 4th KSLI in Normandy,* Major 'Ned' Thornburn, 1990, p 77.
9. Thornburn, p 78.

CHAPTER FOURTEEN

AFTERMATH AND ASSESSMENT

Damage

The Allied high command reacted angrily to Montgomery's apparent failure to break through to Falaise. Tedder caustically noted that at a rate of 1,000 tons of bombs per mile it would take the Army 600,000 tons to reach Berlin. Nevertheless, the Germans recognized the importance of the enlargement of the tiny Orne River bridgehead by nine kilometres, fully securing Caen and establishing a base for 1st Canadian Army to launch the next, inevitable push south. Von Luck's 'thoroughly overtired and battle weary men' were at last able to rest. Of Becker's batteries we hear very little more; when the depleted *21.Panzerdivision* was moved out of the sector, Becker was left behind. Photographic evidence of wrecks supports the view that a considerable number of 'Becker's monsters' were destroyed on the battlefield, and it is reasonable to assume that more became unserviceable due to the lack of standard spare parts in the divisional repair shops. As for the redoubtable *s.Pz.Abt. 503,* 18 July was remembered as the battalion's 'darkest day'. The success of 11 July had briefly upheld the Tiger-men's confidence in their equipment and their unit; after GOODWOOD, von Rosen ruefully reflected, 'for the first time we had the feeling to have failed.' In the words of the battalion historian,

> *...the war there* [in Normandy] *forced us into another dimension that we had not yet known and in which we were inferior. We were crushed in battle by an unimaginable material superiority.*[2]

Strategically, GOODWOOD kept German eyes on the east. The Caen sector remained the hinge of their Normandy defence. To the end of July, a critical period, both *SS-Panzer* corps were held on the German right flank; neither would be able to oppose the American breakout nor support Hitler's Mortain counter-offensive in the west.

Parallels

Comparisons have been drawn between German defensive tactics at GOODWOOD and those developed in the First World War. The defence of the villages on the Bourguébus ridge against tanks has even been likened to the British squares defending the Waterloo slopes against Ney's cavalry.[3]

For decades, GOODWOOD remained a favourite topic for the British Army Staff College battlefield tours. NATO forces, massively outnumbered in Western Europe by the armoured divisions of the Soviet Union, seized upon this example of a small, outnumbered, yet high quality defensive force fending off massed armour. The myth grew that 1944 German tactics held the key to survival, and Staff College invited German veterans of GOODWOOD to talk up their achievements. As late as 1989, battlefield tours were teaching:

> GOODWOOD *proved that armoured forces, in a well-prepared defence, and aggressively led, will prevent any quick penetration, even against very serious odds.*

Optimistic comparisons were made between the 1944 Germans' ten tanks per kilometre in the Caen sector with Northern Army Group's 2,800 MBTs for a front of 220 km. Fortunately for Western Europe, the parallel was not put to the test. By the 1980s the Soviet armoured divisions were equipped with enough armoured infantry and artillery battalions to invalidate comparisons with VIII Corps' tank brigades.

LESSONS

'Pip' Roberts believed that GOODWOOD could have been a decisive British victory had he only taken Cagny when it lay in his grasp. But he cautioned, 'To fight a battle with hindsight is always very easy.'

He admitted that this probably was not a battle in which his infantry brigade could have played a much greater role than they did, since 'I don't think you could have had them trundling along in 3 ton lorries in this very open country.'[4]

However, immediately following GOODWOOD, Roberts initiated training in much closer integration of his tank and infantry brigades, not just at regimental level, but between tank troops and infantry platoons. Instead of their 3 ton lorries, infantry would go into battle riding the tanks. These tactics would be successfully implemented within a fortnight of GOODWOOD, in Operation BLUECOAT. But BLUECOAT is another story.

References

1. von Luck, p 200.
2. Rubbel, p 235.
3. *Six Armies in Normandy,* John Keegan, 1982, ISBN 0 14 00 5293 3, p 213.
4. Roberts, interview at Staff College, Camberley, 1979.

BATTLEFIELD TOURS
AND GENERAL NOTES FOR VISITORS

The countryside around Caen abounds in Second World War battlefields, and the excellent modern road network brings a wide range of accommodation within easy reach, whether urban hotels or rural chambres d'hôte.

The 1:25,000 maps produced by the IGN (*Institut Geographique National*) in the 'Série bleu' are useful guides. The most important is 1512 Est 'CAEN'. Unfortunately, for full coverage of the battlefield area you will also require 1613 Ouest 'BRETTEVILLE-SUR-LAIZE' for the southern sector and 1612 Est 'DIVES-SUR-MER, CABOURG' for the eastern.

Since most of the GOODWOOD battlefield is flat, open country, it is generally possible to view the scene without needing to trespass on farmers' property. Needless to say, entry of the farm complexes such as le Prieuré or le Mesnil Frémentel, or private estates such as the Manneville '*haras*' should not be attempted without first asking permission. As a general rule: if you need to cross any sort of barrier or enter a private farmyard, be prepared to use a few words of French to request permission. Finally, without repeating all the usual safety warnings, keep your eyes open as you go around. The land is full of relics, large and small, from cartridge case to ammunition tin, all bearing witness to the intensity of the battle fought here. Many a farm implement still in use incorporates military hardware.

The following guide suggests two possible starting points for a tour. Cagny stands at the epicentre of the GOODWOOD battle and deserves a visit. However, many visitors will wish to view the excellent Pegasus Bridge museum and one option is to start there. The following recommended routes can be followed either individually, or all together as a single comprehensive tour of the GOODWOOD battlefields.

Recycled wheels from a British carrier.

Cartridge cases.

Ammunition box.

The modern bridge: longer but similiar in design to the original (which remains at the nearby museum).

Tour 1: Pegasus Bridge Museum to Cagny

Just a few minutes' drive south of the Ouistreham ferry port, this excellent museum is found on the eastern side of the pair of bridges captured by the first Allied soldiers to land in Normandy in the early hours of 6 June. (The plaque on the Gondrée café wrongly indicates before midnight; according to both Allied and German Occupation double summer time the landing was made after midnight.) Take time to visit the landing sites of Major Howard's three gliders, tastefully preserved in a garden of remembrance, and marvel at one of the great feats of military aviation.

From the museum, **drive east to a roundabout and turn south** in the direction of **Colombelles**. Pass on your right the brickworks whose chimney is a useful landmark while touring the local landscape. Little remains of the metalworks of the Société Métallurgique de Normandie, whose chimneys used to dominate the whole area. This hardly warrants a visit, so before reaching the large cooling tower, **take a left turn onto the D226**, signed **Cuverville**. After 1.8 km, arriving on the northern side of Cuverville, **turn right at a staggered crossroads** into the village on the **D228**. The 1944 village lay between the road junction and the church ahead, and was totally devastated by the bombing.

As you continue **south towards Démouville**, you are following the route of 3/Monmouths, charged with clearing the villages; to your left you can see the wood taken by the 1/Herefords; the main tank advance passed around the far side of the wood. Modern Démouville bears little resemblance to the 1944 village. As usual, your best guide to the village centre is the church. From that point most of the original village lay 500 metres either side to east and west.

Continuing south, you arrive at a **mini roundabout on the Caen-Troarn** road (the first railway crossed by the tanks ran along the north side of this

road). **Cross over**, and proceed south to cross the A13 *'Autoroute de Normandie'*. If you are able, **pause on the bridge**, or just beyond it, and use its elevation to view the entire width of the armour corridor. Due east, you can make out the Manneville woods where von Rosen's Tiger company was based, and le Prieuré farm with its excellent field of fire. Further right the silos of the modern sugar beet factory behind Cagny are visible. Straight

Cagny church: devastated on 18 July.

ahead along the D228 lie the rooftops of le Mesnil Frémentel, and just before them the surviving hedgerows of la Haie de Saules, where vehicles sheltered and 'Pip' Robert's set up 11th Armoured Tac HQ.

Pressing on along the **road to Cagny**, look out to your left. These were the killing fields where C Squadron of the Fife & Forfars was massacred. **Park in Cagny** to view the rebuilt church and take the short walk to the field, once orchard, where the Flak '88s' were directed by Von Luck.

Tour 2: North of Cagny

Set off from Cagny church in a south-easterly direction, **turning left at the traffic lights** onto the **D225 to Emiéville**. Watch for the stone monument on your left. Neither the wording nor the location of the stone are strictly accurate. The Sherman tank illustrated is a much later model than those available to the Irish Guards in July 1944; nor was *Königstiger 122* the first to be destroyed in Normandy. Standing with your back to the stone, looking due east, the actual ram site is in the left corner of the field ahead. Looking the other way, due west, you can see the gentle slope

187

Distinctive architecture on the N175 at Lirose marks the entrance to the war cemetery.

up which Gorman's tank advanced, following the overhead wires, and if you are feeling fit you can walk down the track to the Ruisseau de Cagny where his tank earlier bogged.

Follow the **D225 to Emiéville, turn left onto the D227** and carry on until you reach a bridge over the motorway, noting as you pass the wall of the Manneville *haras* on your left. With the bridge ahead of you and a modern church on your right (in 2003 condemned as unsafe by order of the small *Mairie* opposite, the civil power scoring points over the church!), **turn left** around the *haras* wall. Passing the main entrance, in 1944 guarded by a large calibre fieldpiece. Carry on around the wall until you come to the main château building on your left. It is worth taking a short walk from this point along the avenue of trees opposite the chateau entrance. Either side of the track are to be seen bomb craters, and from the end you can see le Prieuré ahead. Retracing your path to the motorway, cross over the bridge and **carry on north into Sannerville to meet the N175 Caen-Troarn road**. Turning left, note the fields where *Nebelwerfer* batteries were sited to fire north over the modern rooftops. Just on the western side of **Sannerville**, stop at a small car park from which you can walk to the British War Cemetery. Here are represented most Army units engaged in GOODWOOD. But beware: the dates on the headstones show when soldiers died, not necessarily when they received their wounds. Many of the units represented were long gone by the time their left-behind comrades succumbed. Adjoining the cemetery to the south is the large field where Oemler's *Königstiger* counter-attack was stopped.

After the cemetery, **continue west along the N175**. The single-track railway line is gone but its path, and the little gatekeeper's cottage, remain to this day. Finally, turn left for Cagny or right back to Pegasus Bridge, as you choose.

Tour 3: South of Cagny

With Cagny church on your right, take the **immediate right turn** to leave Cagny **on the little D228**. 1km out of the town you may wish to detour right at the crossroads to view le Prieuré farm, before returning along the same lane to le Mesnil Frémentel. (If you have stout footwear, or strong suspension, you might continue along a rough track to Manneville.) **Backtracking**, follow the Frémentel road as it bends right and passes through the farm complex, then carry straight on westward along a rough track. Note how the road drops away, offering the protection of dead ground against long range fire from Cagny. Reaching the **D230, turn left** following the path of Bill Close's 3/RTR towards Grentheville, over fields where *Nebelwerfer* batteries were emplaced.

Passing **over the railway bridge into Grentheville**, take a **right turn after the church** to reach the elevated railway. Here you may stop and climb the embankment (or if you prefer, walk under the archway!) for a view over the open fields, slanting up to Bourguébus, Hubert-Folie, and distant Bras.

Returning to Grentheville, resume the drive **north through Soliers** where you should **turn right on the D89b for Hubert-Folie**. After driving under the railway bridge, you are retracing the route of David Stileman's carrier section during their high speed recce of Hubert-Folie. Take time around Hubert-Folie and Bras to explore the lanes behind and above the villages, where long range antitank guns were positioned, and to appreciate the amazing fields of fire they enjoyed, until masked by Royal Artillery smoke!

Returning through Bourguébus, pause where the road passes over the railway cutting. This was the high water mark of 3/RTR's 18 July advance. From Bourguébus, **turn left to return to Cagny via Solier**, Four, and le Poirier, guided always by the silos of the Cagny sugar beet factory.

In the Manneville 'haras'.

189

INDEX

OVERLORD, 23

PEOPLE

ALLIES

GERMANS

PLACES